Prayers that Produce Results

PRAYING THE WORD OF GOD

Sis. Bolanle,
It is divine to meet and get to know you. May the Lord bless you and I pray that you will fulfill your destiny in Jesus name.
J. Ekene 4/8/17

Open the Windows of Heaven and Pour out Blessings through Declarations

Prayers that Produce Results

PRAYING THE WORD OF GOD

Josephine Akhagbeme

Copyright © 2016 by Josephine Akhagbeme

All rights reserved. This eBook is protected by the copyright laws of the United States of America. No part of this eBook may be reproduced, stored in a retrieval system or transmitted in any form or by any means without the prior written permission of the author, except for brief quotations.

First electronic publishing.

Published in USA by JOA Ministries.
PO Box 490
Prosper, TX 75078.
joaministries@gmail.com

Unless otherwise indicated, Scripture quotations are taken from The King James Study Bible (previously published as The Liberty Annotated Study Bible and as The Annotated Study Bible, King James Version) Copyright 1988 by Liberty University (KJV).

Scripture taken from the New King James Version® (NKJV). Copyright © 1982 by Thomas Nelson. Used by permission. All rights reserved.

Scripture quotations marked (NLT) are taken from the Holy Bible, New Living Translation, copyright ©1996. Used by permission of Tyndale House Publishers, Inc., Wheaton, Illinois 60189. All rights reserved.

Scriptures taken from **THE HOLY BIBLE, NEW INTERNATIONAL VERSION®, NIV® Copyright © 1973, 1978, 1984, 2011 by Biblica, Inc.® Used by permission. All rights reserved worldwide.**

Scripture quotations taken from the Amplified® Bible (AMP), Copyright © 2015 by The Lockman Foundation Used by permission. www.Lockman.org

Scripture quotation taken from The ESV® Bible (The Holy Bible, English Standard Version®) copyright © 2001 by Crossway, a publishing ministry of Good News Publishers.

Scripture quotations taken from The Living Bible copyright © 1971 by Tyndale House Foundation. Used by permission of Tyndale House Publishers Inc., Carol Stream, Illinois 60188. All rights reserved. The Living Bible, TLB, and The Living Bible logo are registered trademarks of Tyndale House Publishers.

Scripture taken from The Message (MSG). Copyright © 1993, 1994, 1995, 1996, 2000, 2001, 2002. Used by permission of NavPress Publishing Group.

Scripture quotations are from the Revised Standard Version of the Bible (RSV), copyright © 1946, 1952, and 1971 the Division of Christian Education of the National Council of the Churches of Christ in the United States of America. Used by permission. All rights reserved.

Scripture taken from The Voice™. Copyright © 2008 by Ecclesia Bible Society. Used by permission. All rights reserved.

Scripture taken from The ESV® Bible (The Holy Bible, English Standard Version®) copyright © 2001 by Crossway, a publishing ministry of Good News Publishers. ESV® Text Edition: 2011.

Dictionary meaning taken from Merriam Webster's Collegiate Dictionary Tenth Edition copyright © 1993 by Merriam Webster, Incorporated.

eBook published in the United States of America
JOA Ministries
www.joaministries.com
ISBN: 1539521966
ISBN 13: 9781539521969

As the rain and the snow
come down from heaven,
and do not return to it
without watering the earth
and making it bud and flourish,
so that it yields seed for the sower and bread for the eater,
so is my word that goes out from my mouth:
It will not return to me empty,
but will accomplish what I desire
and achieve the purpose for which I sent it.
You will go out in joy
and be led forth in peace;
the mountains and hills
will burst into song before you,
and all the trees of the field
will clap their hands.

Isaiah 55:10-12 (NIV)

I shall not die, but live, and declare the works of the Lord here on earth.

PSALM *118:17*

*This book is dedicated to
all those who seek after the truth of God's Word.*

Contents

Introduction ································· xvii
    Spoken Words ···························· xix
    Vessels of God ···························· xx
    The Prayers in this Book ···················· xxii
    The Elements of Overcoming ················ xxiv
    Evil Mindset ····························· xxvi
    The Victorious Position of Believers ·········· xxix
    Prayer ·································· xxxii

Chapter 1 The Voice of the Lord ··············· 1
    Prayer ···································· 2
    The Battle belong to God ···················· 5
    Prayer ···································· 6
    Spiritual Wilderness ························ 11
    Prayer ··································· 11
    Declaration of Faith ························ 13
    Greatness of God ·························· 15
    Lord of All Lords ·························· 17

Chapter 2 Healing ························· 20
    The Beginning of the Story ·················· 20
    Facts and Truth ··························· 22
    The Enemy's Wrong Label ·················· 25

The Lies of Satan	27
The Finished work of the Cross	30
The End of the Story	30
Shame and Guilt of our Past	31
The Good news of the Gospel	33
Believe – a Major Key to Healing	34
My Healing Story	36
Faith in Prayer	39
Healing Prayer	45
Declaration of Healing	48

Chapter 3 Prayer for Completion of Project(s) and Breakthrough 53

Position yourself for Breakthrough	54
Right Motive in Prayer	56
Praying the Heart of God	58
Leverage the Storms of life to Soar Higher	61
Valley	65
Steps to Breakthrough – Ezekiel 37:1-14	66
Spiritual Storage Graves	68
Prayer	70
Dry Bones Arise	73
Prayer	73
I Prophesy	76
Season of Breakthrough	77
Prayer	77
Advancing God's Kingdom and Righteousness through Tithes and Offering	81
Prayer	83
Blessed in Giving	84
Prayer	84
The Glory of God in my Life	86

	Peace of Jerusalem	88
	Prayer	88
	Prayer for Missionaries	89
Chapter 4	**Restoration**	93
	Steps to Restoration – Deuteronomy 30	94
	Prayer	96
	The Land of the Living	98
	Prayer	99
	Prayer of Restoration	101
	Increase	107
	Prayer	107
	Ministry Supporters	109
	Prayer	109
	Holy Spirit	111
	Prayer	112
Chapter 5	**Ungodly Covenants**	115
	Prayer	118
	Prayer against Evil Pronouncements	121
	Prayer	121
	Curses	123
	Prayer to cancel Curses	125
	Prayer against Unclean Spirits	126
	Thanksgiving	129
	I Have the Mind of Christ	131
	Elohim	132
	Author biography	145
	Blessings of the Seed	149
	Your Right Is Paid For	151

Introduction

One of the weapon we possess as Christians is prayer, and the enemy is not strong enough to take that from us.

~ JOSEPHINE AKHAGBEME

PRAYING IS AN EXERCISE A true Christian cannot avoid. We as Christians, are admonished to "pray constantly and give thanks to God no matter what circumstances we find ourselves in. This is God's will for all of us in Jesus the Anointed."[1] We model our prayer life after our Master Jesus Christ: "During the days of Jesus' life on earth, he offered up prayers and petitions with fervent cries and tears to the one who could save him from death, and he was heard because of his reverent submission. Son though he was, he learned obedience from what he suffered and, once made perfect, he became the source of eternal salvation for all who obey him and was designated by God to be high priest in the order of Melchizedek."[2]

I spent the first thirty-two years of my life in West Africa, Nigeria where I was born. By the time I reached my early adult years, I was

---
1 1 Thessalonians 5:16-18 (VOICE).
2 Hebrews 5:7-10 (NKJV).

already living a promiscuous lifestyle. The words from one of my favorite songs best described my life then:

> "I killed and stole and lied all my life. Tried all I could but didn't get nowhere. Just then I did remember the blood from His side. I applied it and now I am free. What kind of love is this showed by Jesus Christ?"[1]

I was born into a Baptist Christian home but lived a double life playing church. I gave my life to Christ as many times as I backslide. I grew up knowing how to pray because, my mother had nightly devotions with us singing hymns, reading the bible, and praying. By the time I was eighteen, I had memorized several bible verses. I went through all the groups required in the Baptist organization for girls like the Sunbeam, Girl's auxiliary, and Lydia groups. Eventually, it was my mother's ceaseless prayers and unwavering faith, interceding for the salvation of all her children that brought me finally to truly accept Jesus Christ as my Lord and Saviour, in my mid-twenties. By the time I came to America, I had already experienced the power of prayer in so many ways in my life. Not only did the intercessory prayers of my mother affected my life for good, she lived to see all her children come to the saving knowledge of Christ before she passed on to glory.

Years ago, on two different occasions, God spoke to me concerning His Word. In July of 1999 He told me to constantly confess his word audibly; and allow his word to be a part of my daily living by studying and meditating on it because, his word is power and my breakthrough is encapsulated in it. He further told me to confess his word when I encounter any circumstance and difficulty on the way. And as I continue to study and meditate on his word, he will direct my path; and when I commit my desires, plans, and ways unto him, his Holy Spirit will bear witness with God's word in my life to accomplish my desires. He further stated that I should believe because his word is what he stands to perform at all times for it is effective. Similar message came from God to me in January of 2003, God spoke to me when I was praying and asking for His anointing. He said, to pray His Word, preach His Word, and sing His Word; for His Word is healing to my flesh. He said, He will teach me how to pray His Word which is His anointing, Power and Fire that I desire. I have no problem whatsoever believing God because, I have personally experienced what prayers can do in my life and the life of my loved ones – it truly works; for "the effectual fervent prayer of a righteous man availeth much".[3]

Consider these questions: Is your prayer life dormant? Do you notice a pattern of stagnation in your prayer life? Are you struggling to find the right words to pray? Do you want to learn how to pray God's Word with results? Do you desire the enablement of the Holy Spirit to revive your prayer life? Do you desire the fire of the Holy Spirit in your prayer life? This book is written in order to assist you in answering all the above questions and much more. Additionally, this book is written in order to empower you in ascending to a higher spiritual level in prayer. Furthermore, in this book you will learn how to pray with the word of God in faith and belief, prayers that produce results, and praying ceaselessly until the answer comes. Beloved, welcome to my personal prayer journal. I believe with all my heart, when you pray the prayers in this book in faith and belief, you will experience supernatural results in the name of Jesus Christ.

Spoken Words

When it rains, the waters do not return back once it has fallen. It soaks into the ground and nourishes the plants that they grow, thus providing seed to the farmer and food for the hungry. This is similar to God's Word that has been spoken. When God declares something, his Word

---

[3] James 5:16 (KJV).

will go out and not return to him empty or void without results. That Word accomplishes God's desire and achieve the purpose for which it is sent prosperously.[4] God's word when sown in good soil of faith and belief, produces a harvest of abundance of fruit. It is impossible to please God without faith, for any person that comes to God must believe that He exist, and is a rewarder of them that diligently seek Him.[5] Faith must be released and activated by words (the Word of God), and the Kingdom of God is also activated by words (the Word of God). God Himself created all things by His spoken Word; and upholds all things by His Mighty Word of Power.[6] Therefore in order to access the things he has already established, we have to activate them by words, and these words should be the Word of God.

It is crucial to utilize the word of God in prayer because, words remember. Spoken words never forgets its assignment. It may be positive or negative, blessing or cursing; regardless of what you have spoken, it will eventually come to pass. Words can either bind you negatively or positively release you into freedom. They can either put you in the right path toward your destiny or put you in the wrong path away from your destiny. This is why it is so important to be sensitive to the words you speak or words spoken over you. If these words are negative or curses, you should immediately refuse it and cancel it from your life. There are times when we pray and forget however, words declared in prayer will manifest at the appointed time and will not forget its assignment.

Vessels of God

When we pray the word of God, we are aligning ourselves to his will and counsel. In other words, when we pray His Word, He Himself

---

[4] Isaiah 55:8-12.
[5] Hebrews 11:6.
[6] Hebrews 1:3.

accomplishes His Word. In the beginning was the Word, and the Word was with God, and the Word was God.[7] God made a covenant and He is the only one who keeps his covenant. We are only his vessel unto honor, used to accomplish his Word. We do not bring it to pass; only a vessel we will remain. As God's vessels, we are carriers of his power, authority, and anointing. For example: we may be carriers of the songs He wants to release to earth through us for His glory; or carriers of His messages through sermons; or carriers of His Word through books; or His vessels in bringing hope to the hopeless, to prophesy in strengthening, encouraging, and comforting God's people – the church.[8] Regardless of the area He chooses to use us, it is all about Him and his glory and praise. As God's honorable vessels, consecrated and useful to the Master, made ready for every good work He has in store, we ought to clean up our lives and purify ourselves from dishonorable teachings which lead people astray.[9] "Therefore, I urge you, brothers and sisters, in view of God's mercy, to offer your bodies as a living sacrifice, holy and pleasing to God—this is your true and proper worship. Do not conform to the pattern of this world, but be transformed by the renewing of your mind. Then you will be able to test and approve what God's will is—his good, pleasing and perfect will."[10]

You may be wondering, how on earth can anybody seeking an empty vessel, be able to utilize one that is already full? The truth is that, no one can add any additional content to a vessel that is already full. If a vessel is full, you have to look elsewhere for an empty one to use. The only way to keep on using the same vessel over and over again, is to empty its contents and refill it when needed. Sometimes, the contents of a vessel may be kept in the vessel for hours, days, or years, and then

---

7 John 1:1.
8 1 Corinthians 14:3-4.
9 2 Timothy 2:20-22 (VOICE).
10 Romans 12:1-2 (NIV).

emptied. A vessel that has holes, and cannot hold its contents are useless and a waste. May we not be vessels with holes that are useless. May we be vessels unto honor, fit for the Master's use any time he needs us. We ought to constantly pray – help me Lord to remain just the vessel I am created to be, and not the creator. Help me Lord to stay a humble and empty vessel for you to refill and be used over and over to carry out the next assignment, always ready in humility, so help me Lord. This ought to be our daily prayer.

For quite a while now, I have been praying these prayers. The more people that pray these prayers with me, the more formidable we will be against our enemy – Satan and his hosts of wicked demons. We have to fight for our families, our homes, our community, our nation, and our state on our knees. We have to take back through prayer, all that belong to us that the enemy have stolen, "from the days of John the Baptist until now the kingdom of heaven suffers violent assault, and violent men seize it by force [as a precious prize]."[11] Because the Lord is for us, and he has established his covenant with us in His Son Jesus Christ, our enemies will fall before us. Five of us shall chase a hundred, and a hundred of us shall put ten thousand to flight as our enemies fall before us.[12] It is expedient therefore that Christians all over the universe raise their voices up and pray in unity for the battle belongs to God, and the victory has been given unto us. What shall we then say to these things? If God be for us, who can be against us?[13]

THE PRAYERS IN THIS BOOK

I have compiled these prayers not to be limited; it is not an exhaustive list but a guide for us to boldly pray the Word of God in faith and

---

11 Matthew 11:12 (AMP).
12 Leviticus 26:7-9.
13 Romans 8:21 (KJV).

belief. The prayers in this book are personalized, practical, and hands-on, full of thanksgiving and praise because, coming before a Holy God demands that we are free from shame and rejection. The prayers in this book are not focused on our enemy – the devil. How can you fight a defeated opponent that already lost the battle and victory awarded? No, you don't go back and fight a battle where victory has been declared rather, you celebrate that victory. The prayers in this book is a celebration of the victory our Lord Jesus Christ wrought on our behalf on the cross of Calvary. In order for the victorious story to be told, we have to make mention of the loser – Satan. We exalt Jesus Christ for all he has accomplished for us when he died and rose from the grave, hallelujah!

Our victory is linked to the cross of Jesus Christ. All we need for life and godliness is in the cross of Jesus. You cannot enjoy all that God has established for us outside of Christ. You cannot enjoy peace without the Prince of Peace – Jesus Christ; you cannot have joy without Christ, and you cannot love adequately without love himself – Jesus Christ. Nothing absolutely happens outside the cross of Jesus Christ. Indeed, without the cross of Jesus Christ, we are chasing winds. True blessedness is found in the fear of God. In a synopsis, the name of Jesus Christ is so powerful that we cannot extricate it from our prayers. It is the only name, God Almighty decided to put his power and authority on. It is the only name demons obey, the only name that brings fear, chaos, and havoc into the camp of Satan and his demons; the only name that changes atmosphere and produces miracles. And it is the only name that every knee will bow to.[14] Therefore, it is important to pray in the name of Jesus Christ at all times.

> Blessed are all who fear the LORD, who walk in obedience to him. You will eat the fruit of your labor; blessings and prosperity will be yours. Your wife will be like a fruitful vine within

---

14 Philippians 2:10-12.

your house; your children will be like olive shoots around your table. Yes, this will be the blessing for the man who fears the LORD. May the LORD bless you from Zion; may you see the prosperity of Jerusalem all the days of your life. May you live to see your children's children—peace be on Israel.[15]

The Word of God admonishes us to pray constantly and tirelessly – without ceasing[16] as we encounter situations and circumstances beyond our control. I will enter his gates with thanksgiving, and into his courts with praise. Lord, I am thankful unto you and bless your Holy name.[17] You've got to profess the word of God audibly, consistently, and nonstop over your situation until you see results. There are so many scriptures in the bible not listed in this book, you can locate and apply them to your life. "If I shut up heaven that there be no rain says the Lord, or if I command the locusts to devour the land, or if I send pestilence among my people; if my people, which are called by my name, shall humble themselves, and pray, and seek my face, and turn from their wicked ways; then will I hear from heaven, and will forgive their sin, and will heal their land. Now, mine eyes shall be open, and mine ears attend unto the prayer that is made in this place - wherever you are.[18]

The Elements of Overcoming

We as Christians serve a supernatural God. Everything about our God is supernatural "And these signs shall follow them that believe; In my name, shall they cast out devils; they shall speak with new tongues; They shall take up serpents; and if they drink any deadly thing, it shall

---

15 Psalm 128 (NIV).
16 1 Thessalonians 5:17.
17 Psalm 100:4.
18 2 Chronicles 7:13-15 (KJV).

not hurt them; they shall lay hands on the sick, and they shall recover.[19] Regardless of what we see or experience, prayers can reverse the FACT to align with the "TRUTH" of God's Word. We can change situations and circumstances that are contrary through prayers. This is how powerful and formidable the prayers of saints are. The elements of overcoming are: declaring God's word in faith, belief, and offering forgiveness.[20] I believe with all my heart when you pray the prayers in this book in faith, truth, and belief; it will produce results. I have experienced these results in different areas of my life and I know, you will too.

In Luke 1:26-38, the angel Gabriel was sent from God unto the Virgin Mary, to tell her about the coming miracle; and that, she had found favor with God and was about to be the mother of Jesus, the Son of God. After the angel told her what was to happen, Mary's response proved she was a mature Christian who had a personal relationship with God. "And Mary said behold the handmaid of the Lord; be it unto me according to thy word" Mary instantly received the word she was given in faith. She believed God's word. And in verse 45, it says "And blessed is she that believed: for there shall be a performance of those things which were told her from the Lord." You have to first believe what the Word of God says for it to be accomplished. The Bible talks about a person who doubts the Word of God, such a one will not receive anything from God: "But when you ask, you must believe and not doubt, because the one who doubts is like a wave of the sea, blown and tossed by the wind. That person should not expect to receive anything from the Lord."[21]

Hezekiah was a king who was sick unto death. God Himself confirms that he will die and not live. He was a man of faith who would not settle for the verdict of death upon his life even though it came

---

19 Mark 16:16-18 (KJV).
20 Mark 11:22-26.
21 James 1:6-7 (NIV).

from God through His prophet. He immediately took action in prayer. He reminded God of how he walked before him in truth and with a perfect heart. He reminded him of the good he had done in his sight. He came before the Almighty God with a broken and contrite heart; and in repentance and humility, he cried unto the Lord to spare his life. God, who is Merciful and Gracious, heard his prayers, healed him, and added fifteen more years to his life.[22] For with The True God of heaven we serve, nothing shall be impossible.[23] "Here's what I want to see: Men, pray wherever you are. Reach your holy hands to heaven—without rage or conflict—completely open. Women, the same goes for you: (and in addition), dress properly, modestly, and appropriately. Don't get carried away in grooming your hair or seek beauty in glittering gold, pearls, or expensive clothes."[24] Let everyone therefore, lift up their voices in unity and pray that the Lord of hosts will fight for us and manifest the victory he has already established on the cross of Calvary.

Evil Mindset

It is very important to be watchful against the suggestions from the enemy that comes through human thoughts, for "unto the pure all things are pure: but unto them that are defiled and unbelieving is nothing pure; but even their mind and conscience is defiled."[25] You must realize that the power of Satan and his demons are through the thoughts of humans and if he succeeds, it becomes a wicked evil mindset. The effective way to tear down the stronghold of this wicked demonic mindset erected against God's truth is to bring it to God in prayer and: demolish arguments and ideas, every high-and-mighty philosophy that

---

22 2 Kings 20:1-11.
23 Luke 1:37.
24 1 Timothy 2:8-9 (VOICE).
25 Titus 1:15 (KJV).

pits itself against the knowledge of the one true God, take prisoners of every thought, every emotion, and subdue them into obedience to the Anointed One – Jesus Christ of Nazareth.[26]

When these evil and defeated fallen enemies of humanity succeeds in planting the seed of evil thoughts of (hatred, fear, doubt, suicide, hopelessness, unbelief, depression, insecurity, anger, unforgiveness, etc.), it becomes a stronghold and if you continue to entertain it, it turns into a mindset, and eventually begin to believe the lies of Satan as true. This my beloved, is the direct voices of demonic oppression. In talking about how a stronghold is built in a person's life, Schnoebelen (1994) suggested:

> *It begins from a sinful thought that is caused by either our flesh, the environment, or Satan's servants. If not resisted, it leads to a sinful choice; and if this is repeated often enough, it leads to a sinful habit. This is where the stronghold begins to be constructed out of the flesh or sin nature. If not resisted, this habit leads to loss of control. Here, the person no longer has a clear choice whether to sin or not and this is where the demonic element begins to really take hold. If not stopped, it leads to bondage. Here, the strongman has taken residence in the stronghold and the person is demonically bound. If there is no spiritual intervention, it transitions to total control. This category is rare or virtually impossible for Christians to experience. In a Christian, it would be the most serious form of demon oppression imaginable. However, in a non-Christian, this will be demon possession (pp. 67-68).*[ii]

You have to constantly counter these lies with the word of God. Guard your heart and your thoughts; "always think on things that are true, honest, just, pure, lovely, and of good report; if there be any virtue,

---

26 2 Corinthians 10:4-6 (VOICE).

and any praise, think on these things."[27] You have to constantly engage a proactive and intentional process of audible declaration of God's word against the thoughts you hear in your heads. They are the voices of Satan and his demons, and these are all lies. For example, a person who did not create himself is able to claim he is more superior than any other; or no other life matters other than theirs; or wishing that certain groups of people should be completely annihilated from the face of the earth, as they continue to make several excuses to justify their wicked depraved actions.

Many Christians short change themselves on this earth. God has established fruitful life for his children on earth before they make it to their permanent abode in heaven. In speaking to the priestly nation of Israel, the Lord said "my people are destroyed for lack of knowledge."[28] This truth is evident in our generation today as well. It is a noble goal to make it to heaven however, God desire to use his children effectively on earth to impact our world and win souls into his kingdom, before graduating into his presence.

As Christians, we must not be satisfied with just making it to heaven, we should desire to do more for the kingdom of God here on earth first. God has given us all of heaven's resources to carry out our purpose and achieve our destiny on earth. He has given us his authority and power through the name of Jesus Christ and the Holy Spirit. He has given us his weapon of his word – which is also the sword of the Spirit.[29] "For the word of God is living and active *and* full of power [making it operative, energizing, and effective]. It is sharper than any two-edged sword, penetrating as far as the division of the soul and spirit [the completeness of a person], and of both joints and marrow [the deepest parts of our nature], exposing *and* judging the very thoughts and intentions of

---

27 Philippians 4:8 (KJV).
28 Hosea 4:6.
29 Ephesians 6:17.

the heart."[30] He has given us all that we need for life and godliness, and great treasure for his kingdom sake. He has given us healing in order to enjoy good health to carry out his work longer. He has given us the power over Satan to bind him and stop his wicked schemes.[31]

The Victorious Position of Believers

We are operating from the position of victory over any obstacle that will hinder us on earth. The sad truth is that; Satan is aware of his defeated position. But his strategy is to calibrate and operate on the ignorance of God's children with his convoluted evil agenda. He is getting away with it because God's people are not aware of their victorious position. Satan does not want Christians to know that they are victorious and overcomers in Christ. He will rather keep the church in ignorance and in a cul-de-sac position of ineffective and unproductive Christian living. The good news is that joy and victory has been given to believers "Shouts of joy and victory resound in the tents of the righteous: "The Lord's right hand has done mighty things!""[32]

No situation is stronger than any prayer offered in faith and belief. Such prayer is a breath of life from God and can never be wasted. Nothing is wasted in God's hands. One of the reason this book is so important to the body of believers is that, the prayers are rendered from a victorious higher position in Christ. When you are cognizant of your victorious position, your mindset changes and you begin to approach God with a settled belief. Your prayers begin to shift from the position of a beggar to that of ownership; from a servant to that of a son; from slave to master; from orphan to joint-heir of the kingdom of God; from

---

30 Hebrews 4:12 (AMP).
31 Luke 10:19.
32 Psalm 118:15 (NIV).

outcast and downcast to God's beloved; from defeat to victory; from fear to boldness; from insecurity to authority and power.

Knowing your position in Christ is one of the crucial element in praying with results. Your overcoming victory is not determined by the trials you encounter in life. In other words, you may be going through trials and tribulations in so many ways however, in actuality you are an overcomer whose ultimate victory is guaranteed. As Christians, we have been raised up together, and we sit together in heavenly places in Christ Jesus.[33] We approach God in relationship from within and not from the outside. He is now our Father and we are his beloved children. we are loved, we are accepted, we are needed and wanted, we are no longer outcasts, no longer cast down, no longer orphans but children of the Most High. Understanding this position helps us to pray with boldness to receive all God has already manifested for us.

The prayers in this book are only for believers who have accepted Jesus Christ as their personal Lord and Saviour, and these are those that belong to the kingdom of God. "He that believeth and is baptized shall be saved; but he that believeth not shall be damned.[34] Grace is extended to all however; truth of God's word will not be compromised whatsoever.[35] As a Christian, you have to know your identity in Jesus Christ, with the understanding that you are operating in the authority of God as given unto you by Jesus Christ. You have been given the power to thread on serpents and scorpions and over all the powers of the enemy, and nothing by any means will injure you.[36] This authority can only be exerted in obedience to God through prayer. Prayer is the only key to accessing this power of authority from God. The bible admonishes us to

---

33 Ephesians 2:6.
34 Mark 16:16 (KJV).
35 John 1:14, 17
36 Luke 10:19.

pray always with all prayer and supplications. Prayer is essential in this ongoing warfare. Pray hard and long. Pray for your brothers and sisters. Keep your eyes open. Keep each other's spirits up so that no one falls behind or drops out.[37] Only those who are born again can be heard by God for "The Lord is far from the wicked, but he hears the prayer of the righteous."[38] Furthermore, "the curse of the Lord is in the house of the wicked: but he blesses the habitation of the just."[39]

If you do not have this personal relationship with God Almighty – The Creator of the universe, I invite you right now to ask Him into your heart so you can access his immeasurable vastness of goodness and mercy. Accepting Jesus as your Lord is the only way you can be a part of God's kingdom to effectively pray the prayers in this book in faith and experience results. The kingdom of God is not a realm of grandiose talk; it is a realm of power.[40] The only way to access God's power is through Jesus Christ: "that if you confess with your mouth the Lord Jesus and believe in your heart that God has raised Him from the dead, you will be saved. For with the heart one believes unto righteousness, and with the mouth confession is made unto salvation.[41] Pray with me now:

Jesus, I have heard your word. I confess that I am a sinner in need of a Savior. I understand that, no one can come to you unless the Father who sent you draws him; and you will raise him up at the last day.[42] I therefore come to you in humility to ask for your forgiveness. Forgive me of my sins of (name known sins). Forgive me of all the wrong I have done. Have mercy on me – a sinner. I repent and willingly turnaround from my wicked ways. I renounce my allegiance to Satan from this day

---

37 Ephesians 6:18 (MSG).
38 Proverbs 15:29 (NIV).
39 Proverbs 3:33 (KJV).
40 1 Corinthians 4:20 (VOICE).
41 Romans 10:9-10 (NKJV).
42 John 6:44-45.

forward. Come into my life and be my Master and Lord. Empower me by your Holy Spirit to pray these prayers in faith and belief as I expect results according to your word. I do not understand all things but I choose to put my trust in your Holy Spirit who will reveal the truth of God's Word to my heart.[43] I thank you that I am forgiven in Jesus name, amen!

Prayer

Father, we are limited in our finitude to understand and comprehend your awesomeness and greatness. I ask that you would reveal unto me the abundance of peace and truth.[44] As I call unto you this day, answer and show me great and mighty things I do not know or understand[45] by your Spirit who is the revealer of secrets and the Spirit of truth.[46] You have established your victory in my life. You know me by name for I have found grace in your sight. You shaped and formed me, inside and out. You knitted me together in my mother's womb long before I took my first breath. I offer you my grateful heart, for I am your unique and special creation, filled with wonder and awe. You have approached even the smallest details with excellence; your works are wonderful; I carry this knowledge deep within my soul. My Father, you see all things; nothing about me was hidden from you as I took shape in the secret of my mother's womb, carefully crafted in the heart of the earth before I was born from its womb.[47]

My Father, I thank you for the authority I have as your child. I bind all wicked spirits that will hinder these prayers in anyway, and I

---

43 Daniel 2:47, John 16:13-14.
44 Jeremiah 33:6.
45 Jeremiah 33:3.
46 John 14:17, 26-27.
47 Psalm 139:12-15 (VOICE).

bind any demonic stronghold of faithlessness and unbelief that want to take over my heart as I pray in the name of Jesus Christ. I loose God's presence around me. I loose all that I will declare in these prayers to manifest and align with heaven in Jesus name, amen.[48] I saturate the atmosphere around me with the blood of Jesus Christ.

My Father, by the power of your Holy Spirit, I have come to declare and align with what you came to accomplish for me which is: healing, freedom, deliverance, and comfort. For you have given unto me beauty for ashes, the oil of joy for mourning, the garment of praise for the spirit of heaviness; that I might be called a tree of righteousness and the planting of the Lord, that he might be glorified.[49] I shall be named the priest of the Lord; men shall call me the servant of our God; I will feed on the wealth of the nations, and in their riches, I will boast. Instead of shame, I will receive a double portion, and instead of disgrace I will rejoice in my inheritance. I will inherit a double portion in my land, and everlasting joy will be mine. I am blessed because I delight greatly in the Lord; my soul rejoices in my God. For he has clothed me with garments of salvation and arrayed me in a robe of righteousness.[50]

My Father, as I come into your presence, I will not be anxious about things, instead, I will keep on praying and trusting in your Word of truth. I will pray all manner of prayers with thanksgiving. As I bring my requests before you, I know that the peace of God which is beyond all human understanding will continually stand watch over my heart and mind in Christ Jesus my Lord, amen![51] I choose to rejoice in the Lord my God always. I thank you Father, for you are constantly present in my life and situation. Therefore, I thank you for answering me before I

---

48 Matthew 18:18.
49 Isaiah 61:1-3.
50 Isiah 61:6-10.
51 Philippians 4:4-7.

call, and while I am still talking to you about my needs, you have gone ahead and answered my prayers.[52]

Lord, I am full of expectancy for what you about to accomplish in my life this season. Lord, I have the victory, for surely, there is an end and my expectation shall not be cut off.[53] Let the words of my mouth, and the meditation of my heart, be acceptable in thy sight, O LORD, my strength, and my redeemer.[54] Teach me to number my days that I may gain a heart of wisdom by your Holy Spirit. Satisfy me in the morning with your unfailing love that I may sing for joy and be glad all my days. May the favor of the Lord my God and His beauty and grace, continue to rest upon me all the days of my life and bring me good success in all I do.[55] I thank you Father, for your presence and glory in our midst separates us from everyone else[56] in Jesus name I pray, amen! I apply the blood of Jesus Christ over me and my loved ones for our wholeness in Jesus name.

---

52 Isaiah 65:23-25.
53 Proverbs 23:18.
54 Psalm 19:14.
55 Psalm 90:12-17.
56 Exodus 33:14-18.

CHAPTER 1

The Voice of the Lord

*The Spirit of God is speaking but the church is not listening.
Align to the supernatural realm, tune in to the voice of the
Spirit in prayer, and experience the miraculous.*

~ JOSEPHINE AKHAGBEME

ALL THINGS IN THE KINGDOM of God are voice activated. Declarations are made audibly from our mouths. You call things that are not with your mouths as though they are – because in truth and actuality, they exist already. I love to pray these prayers audibly because, not only does it build my faith in God, but the devil and his demons, who cannot read my mind will be able to hear these declarations and obey the voice of God. You will decide and decree a thing, and it shall be established for you; and the light of God's favor will shine upon your ways.[57] All that we need for life and godliness already exist and made available for all believers, and this comes only through the full personal knowledge of Him Who called us by and to His own glory and excellent virtue.[58] In order for these blessings to be made manifest and accessible, we have to

---

57 Job 22:28.
58 2 Peter 1:3.

call them forth by faith. Faith is having a settlement and belief in your heart that, what God have spoken is true and it actually exist. Having this settled belief in your heart produces confidence and boldness to come into his presence. To align with God's word that exist already, you will have to declare it into manifestation in your life by faith. God is bound by his word and when declared in faith, it will produce results.

The enemy's plan is to stifle God's voice in your life. He distracts God's people in so many ways in order to compete for your attention and compete for the righteous seed God planted in your life to bear righteous fruit for his glory and praise. His goal is to compete for God's presence in your life with the intention of getting the praise he so desperately craves. He wants to distract you from hearing the voice of the Lord. He brings all sorts of distractions that sometimes seems good and with a pretense of contributing to the work of God. It is so important therefore, for believers to be discerning and sensitive to the voice of the Spirit of God. It is also important to be connected to God in prayer; "My sheep hear my voice, and I know them, and they follow me: And I give unto them eternal life; and they shall never perish, neither shall any man pluck them out of my hand."[59]

Prayer

Father in the name of Jesus Christ of Nazareth, I come into your presence Most Excellent King. I come into the courts of heaven by the blood of the Lamb, and the name of Jesus Christ, to offer these prayers unto you – my King. Your Excellency, I come before the splendor of Your Majesty. I honor and reverence your name lifting you up: for you Oh Lord our God is Holy.[60] I give you all glory and strength that is due unto your Holy name. I worship you Elohim, Majestic is your name in

---

59 John 10:27-28 (KJV).
60 Psalm 99:9 (NIV).

all the earth. I come before your beauty of Holiness bowing before Your Majesty. I have come to declare these prayers in faith and belief, not by my power or strength, but by the empowerment of the Holy Spirit, for none of these prayers will be lost. Holy Spirit, you are my helper. Come and help me to pray God's will, for I do not know what I should pray as I ought. Come and make intercession for me according to the will of God.[61] My Father, as these prayers ascend unto your presence as sweet smelling savor, may you watch over your words and perform them with signs and wonders following in Jesus name.

Lord, as I come into your presence to pray, forgive me of every sin I may have committed in words, in deed, or in action, knowingly or unknowingly, by commission or omission. Forgive me for any inner vows I may have made; forgive me for every negative and idle words I have spoken out of my lips that will give the devil a legal ground against me; forgive me for (name known sin); forgive me for doing things my own way; forgive me for faithlessness, unbelief, fear, and anxiety; forgive me for any critical and judgmental attitude in my heart; forgive me for all anger and unforgiveness I may have harbored in my heart; forgive me for all pride and arrogance in my heart;[62] forgive me for every racism or tribalism that may exist in my heart; I repent for any failures I've had in my life in any capacity. I repent for accepting the lies of the enemy over my life. I repent of any vain imaginations I may have entertained. Forgive me of any insecurity I have in my life. Forgive me for any actions, attitudes, and words I may have given the accuser to bind me with; forgive me for stealing from you through tithes and offerings.[63]

Have mercy on me, O God, according to your steadfast love; according to your abundant mercy. Create in me a clean heart, O God, and put a new and right spirit within me. Father, I thank you for blotting

---

61 Romans 8:26-27.
62 Proverbs 8:13.
63 Malachi 3:9-11.

out my transgressions and washing me thoroughly from my iniquity[64] and cleansing me from all sin. Restore to me the joy of your salvation, and sustain in me a willing spirit.[65] Thank you Lord for you have not dealt with me after my sins, nor rewarded me according to my iniquities. For as the heaven is high above the earth, so great is your mercy toward me that fear you. As far as the east is from the west, so far have you removed my transgressions from me.[66]

I have acknowledged my sin (of missing the mark), and did not cover up my iniquity (premeditated and habitual sin). I have confessed my transgressions (willful sin) to you my Lord, and I thank you that you have forgiven the guilt of my sin.[67] Empower me from this day forward to start honoring you through my tithes and offerings so I can be blessed, and to access your provision and your divine protection in all areas of my life.

My Father, empower me to begin to do the right thing and obey your word. Anoint me with fresh oil.[68] May my life be unto you, a sweet fragrance of Christ.[69] My Father, may you be unto me like refreshing dew from heaven. May I continue to blossom like the lily. May the root of holiness continue to go deeper into the soil of my soul as the cedars of Lebanon. May I continue to live under your shade of glory. May I continue to flourish like grain and blossom like grapevines. May I be as fragrant as the wines of Lebanon by the empowerment of your Holy Spirit.[70] I praise and thank you in Jesus name, amen.

---

64 Isaiah 53:3
65 Psalm 51 (NRSV).
66 Psalm 103:10-12.
67 Psalm 32:5.
68 Psalm 92:10.
69 2 Corinthians 2:15.
70 Hosea 14:4-7 (NLT).

My Father, I will not be anxious about anything, but trust you who knows all things and is aware of all my needs. By prayer and supplication with thanksgiving, I offer these prayers and requests unto you. And the peace of God, which is beyond all understanding, shall keep my heart and mind through Christ Jesus. My Father, I understand that anxiety can hinder prayers and it is tied to unbelief and faithlessness, and anything that is not of faith is sin.[71] I therefore choose to dwell and think on things that are true, honest, just, pure, lovely, excellent, praise worthy, and have virtue in them.[72] I thank you my Father, for there is no want to them that fear you.[73] I thank you Elohim, that there is nothing impossible with you.[74] Father, it is not about me but, it is all about your glory, your power, your anointing, your grace, your goodness, your favor, your blessings, your work, and your kingdom in my life. It is all about you, Your Majesty; it is about your name. And because it is all about you, the words I utter in prayer will manifest and produce results in the name of Jesus Christ. I apply the blood of Jesus Christ over me and my loved ones for our wholeness in Jesus name.

The Battle belong to God

As Christians in our spiritual walk, we encounter trials, tribulations, temptations, and all sorts of battles intended to derail, discourage, and hinder us from all sides. These battles we face daily are engineered by the devil and his demons using humans as his tools. "For we are not fighting against people made of flesh and blood, but against persons without bodies—the evil rulers of the unseen world, those mighty satanic beings and great evil princes of darkness who rule this world;

---

71 Romans 14:23.
72 Philippians 4:6-8.
73 Psalm 34:9.
74 Luke 1:37.

and against huge numbers of wicked spirits in the spirit world."[75] If we believe that the battle indeed belongs to the Lord, how do we hand over these battles to him? You can only accomplish this by faith. If we trust God that He is able to do all he says, we ought to trust him with our relationships, our trials, our tribulations, and our pains. For we know in whom we believed, and are persuaded that he is able to keep that which we have committed unto him against that day."[76] The Lord God released his creative word and spoke this universe into existence. Begin to align with that creative word of God and release it in faith and belief over any situation and circumstances you are faced with right now. "Is there anything too hard for God?"[77] "For with God, nothing shall be impossible."[78]

Prayer

Father, it is not for me to fight my battle neither is it for me to contend with the enemy. You have already fought and won the battle on my behalf, establishing the victory for me. You have spoken that in you I will have peace, but the world is full of trouble. I rejoice because, you have overcome the world on my behalf.[79] Lord I thank you for given me the authority to trample on snakes and scorpions and to overcome all the administrative power, and fury, and ability of the enemy; and nothing whatsoever will harm me.[80] I thank you for restoring my dominion of rule and authority in Christ, which was lost to Satan at the fall when

---

75 Ephesians 6:12 (TLB).
76 2 Timothy 1:12.
77 Jeremiah 32:27.
78 Luke 1:37 (KJV).
79 John 16:33.
80 Luke 10:19-20 (NIV).

Adam and Eve disobeyed you.[81] I thank you Lord for the battle is yours. I can do nothing without your Mighty power – for you are all powerful, and I can do nothing without Your Holy Spirit.

My Father, begin to demonstrate your miraculous power in my life with signs and wonders following because "the kingdom of God is not in word but in excessive Power; not in man's wisdom, but in demonstration of the Spirit and His Miraculous Power.[82] I thank you my Father, for though we live in our fleshly bodies, we do not fight in the physical: For the weapons of our warfare are not weapons of flesh and blood, but they are mighty in God for pulling down strongholds, casting down arguments and theories and reasoning and every proud and lofty thing that sets itself up against the true knowledge of God; and we lead every thought and purpose away captive into the obedience of Christ – the Messiah, the Anointed One.[83]

Jehovah God, Your voice thunders over the mighty waters. Your voice Oh God is like a noise of many waters.[84] Your voice Oh Most Holy One strikes with flashes of lightning. Your voice Oh Lord is Majestic. As my battle axe and weapon of war,[85] let the voice of the Lord rise up and begin to make war for me. My King, you are the Mighty Warrior. You are mighty in battle; Majestic is your splendor of Holiness. You are God, and there is none else. You are God and there is none like you. The battle is thine alone and you have declared the victory way ahead of the battle. You have declared the end from the beginning, and my end resounds with victory. From beginning you declare how things will end; and tell what is yet to be. For your intentions, will come to pass

---

81 Genesis 3:1-7.
82 1 Corinthians 2:4; 4:20.
83 2 Corinthians 10:4-5 (AMP).
84 Ezekiel 43:2.
85 Jeremiah 51:20.

and you will make things happen as you determine they should.[86] And I am confident that God is able to orchestrate everything to work toward something good and beautiful in my life because I love Him and accept His invitation to live according to His plan.[87]

Father, begin to destroy false arguments, imaginations, and all high things that exalts itself against the knowledge of God in my life; bringing into captivity every thought to the obedience of Christ Jesus. I therefore put on me, all the protective armor of God – The Belt of Truth; The Breastplate of righteousness; strapped to my feet are the Sandals of Peace; The Shield of Faith in extinguishing the flaming arrows of the evil one; The Helmet of Salvation; and The Sword of the Spirit, which is the Word of God.[88] Every evil spirit and household demons coming against me, and every negative and ungodly mindset be bound, and I command you to align to the mind of Christ, in the name of Jesus.

Your Majesty let your voice, your Powerful voice break into pieces in my life, every valley of stagnation, every valley of fear and doubt, every valley of anxiety and stress, every valley of faithlessness and unbelief, every valley of mounting debts, every valley of clouded vision that has blurred my purpose and destiny, every mountain of degeneration, every mountain of sicknesses and diseases, every mountain of mental illness, every mountain of oppression and depression, every mountain of injustice and wickedness, every mountain of poverty and lack, every mountain of confusion and misplaced priorities, every mountain of procrastination and laziness, and every mountain of lack of strength, vigor, and excessive weight, that has hindered my destiny. For my sake, you are coming down in the name of Jesus Christ of Nazareth. Who art thou, O great mountain? Before me you

---

86 Isaiah 46:9-10 (VOICE).
87 Romans 8:28 (VOICE).
88 Ephesians 6:14-18.

shall become a plain, leveled to the ground. With shouts of Grace! Grace! You are coming down, and with shouts of Peace! Peace! You are coming down.[89] With shouts of Victory! Victory! You are coming down in the name of Jesus Christ of Nazareth. Because, "As the righteous soldier of God, shouts of joy and victory resound in my home and dwelling place. The hand of GOD has turned the tide! The hand of GOD is raised in victory on my behalf!"[90]

My Father, let your mighty powerful voice dislocate every barrier in my path to greatness; and every hindrance that will hinder your glory from being revealed in my life in the name of Jesus. Let your voice break and destroy all spiritual wedges and hedges in my life in the name of Jesus Christ of Nazareth. By your power, I am rising up in victory above every situation trying to choke me, and every circumstance trying to hinder me. I am rising above every obstacle trying to hinder the effectiveness of God's power in my life. I am rising above every controversy and disunity, for the Lord is pleading my case.[91] I am rising above the tide of debt that is trying to hinder my progress. I am rising above every voice of opposition and injustice trying to silent me. I am rising above every voice of accusation raised against me. I am rising above every hindrance trying to overcome me because you Elohim are Lord over all. My Father, you deliver the poor in his affliction, and open their ears in oppression.[92] Elohim, as I delight myself in you, the desires of my heart are granted.[93] Father, there is no want to them that fear you. Lord, because I seek you, I shall not want any good thing.[94] Your blessings makes my life rich and

---

89 Zechariah 4:6-8.
90 Psalm 118:15-16 (MSG).
91 Micah 6:2.
92 Job 36:15.
93 Psalm 37:4.
94 Psalm 34:9-10.

adds no sorrow with it.⁹⁵ You are Lord over everything that exists, and over every power that be, therefore, I am not afraid.

My King, let your voice begin to divide the unity of your enemies just like you divide the flames of fire. Let your voice as lightning scatter their gatherings with confusion. Let your lightning Most Holy One reveal every dark hidden secret and agenda of the wicked; you will bring to light what is hidden in darkness and expose the motives of the heart.⁹⁶ Let your voice Majestic One, begin to split and disperse the camp of the wicked in the name of Jesus Christ. Lord, curse everything that murmurs in my life, and bind the murmuring spirit of unbelief that is operating around me in the name of Jesus Christ. Lord, cause every contrary voice of guilt and condemnation against me to be permanently silenced in Jesus name.

I begin to declare peace and quietness in my life and home. I am blessed when I come in and when I go out. The Lord will cause my enemies who rise against me to be defeated before me. When they come against me one way, they will flee before me seven different ways in confusion in the name of Jesus Christ.⁹⁷ I am an overcomer, and I overcome the devil by the blood of the Lamb, and the word of my testimony.⁹⁸ I have redemption through the blood of Jesus Christ, the forgiveness of sins according to the riches of His grace.⁹⁹ The Lord has commanded his blessing upon my life and all that I undertake. He will surely bless me in this land of the living in the name of Jesus Christ.¹⁰⁰ I apply the blood of Jesus Christ over me and my loved ones for our wholeness in Jesus name.

---

95 Proverbs 10:22.
96 1 Corinthians 4:5.
97 Deuteronomy 28:25.
98 Revelation 12:11.
99 Ephesians 1:7.
100 Deuteronomy 28:6-8.

Spiritual Wilderness

Prayer

I was dead in my transgression and sin in which I used to live as a sinner following the ways of this world and the ruler of the kingdom of the air - the evil spirit who now possesses and operate in the lives of those who are disobedient. Like everyone, I was by nature deserving the wrath of a Merciful and Just God. Because of His great love for us, God who is rich in mercy, made us alive in His Son – Jesus Christ even as sinners. It is by His grace through faith that I have been saved. This is not my doing rather; it is the gift of God that does not come by works, so that no one can boast. I therefore declare, that I am God's handiwork, created in Christ Jesus to do good works, which God prepared in advance for me to do.[101]

The Lord created me, therefore, I shall not fear. For the Lord, have redeemed me and called me by my name, I am His beloved. He has given me new names of: *saved, redeemed, heir of eternal life, beloved, forgiven, led by the Spirit, new creature, holy, blessed, prosperous, precious, highly favored, apple of his eye, chosen, peculiar, renown, famous, honored, memorable, flourishing, victorious, glorious, sanctified, overcomer, healed, delivered, transformed, conqueror, obedience, faithful, joyful and delightful, married, and righteous.*[102iii] When I pass through the waters, he will be with me; and through the rivers, it shall not overflow me. When I walk through the fire of persecution and trials, I shall not be burnt; neither shall the flame destroy me. For the Lord my God, the Holy One of Israel, my Saviour is with me.[103] The Lord is faithful and will keep his promise. The plans he has for me are for peace, not evil, to give me a future and

---

101 Ephesians 2:1-11 (NIV).
102 Isaiah 62:2.
103 Isaiah 43:1-3.

hope of an expected end. As I call upon the Lord, he will hear; and as I pray unto him, he will listen and answer me.[104]

My Father, let your Powerful voice make every wilderness in my life tremble just like you shake the wilderness of Kadesh. Mighty One let your voice thunder from Your Throne over the wilderness in my life. Let the voice of the Lord thunder over every area and dark recess of my life, all the uninhabited parts of my life, all the wasteland of my soul, all the desolate and unchecked corners of my life. Let the voice of the Lord begin to shake them right now. Let the voice of the Lord begin to cause His life to flow into me as they are being shaken. Let the voice of the Lord begin to fill all uninhabited areas in my life with His Majestic presence. Let the Powerful voice of His Majesty begin to flood all the uncultivated region of my soul with His Love, Peace, Joy, Holiness, Righteousness, and Praise. As He saturate me, let every wasteland become fertile ground in my life, useful for God's service. Let all the deserted parts of my life begin to spring up with life. Let every part of me begin to luxuriantly grow with the fragrance of The Holy One. Lord, as you shake the wilderness of my life, may they begin to tremble before you and yield to your authority in the name of Jesus Christ of Nazareth.

Lord, thank you for going ahead of your people in victory. Mighty One, you declare the end from the beginning. Man of War, you have given your children the victory way ahead of the battle. Your ears are open to the cry of your children O Most Holy One. Because I am blessed by the Lord, I will possess this land (name of your town) where my feet are planted. The Lord directs my steps and He delights in every detail of my life. Though I stumble, I will never fall, for the Lord holds me by the hand. My Father, the abundance belongs to you, the increase and the promotion comes from you. It pleases you to bless me and give me of your abundance and increase as the seed of Abraham in Jesus

---
104 Jeremiah 29:10-12.

Christ.[105] Once I was young, and now I am old, I have never seen the righteous abandoned or their children begging for bread.[106] I will not worry about my life, what I will eat or drink, or what to put on. Just as the Lord feeds the birds of the air, and clothe the grass of the field, He will clothe and feed me as well, because He is a good Father.[107] I apply the blood of Jesus Christ over me and my loved ones for our wholeness in Jesus name.

DECLARATION OF FAITH

I bless you Jehovah; your name is mighty in all the earth. You are powerful, you are great, and you are marvelous. Take all the praise and glory forever and ever, amen! You are great O God, and not made by human hands. I bow before Your Majesty, I worship you, and there is no God like you in all the earth. I bow my knees before you; I bless your Holy name. I believe in you and I believe all the promises of God in Christ Jesus are yea and amen.[108] I believe in *the inerrancy of the Word of God that it is inspired, accurate, reliable, authoritative, and without error* (Towns, 2008, p. 29).[iv] I believe in the Triune God – God the Father, God the Son, and God the Holy Spirit, and they are united together in one purpose.[109] I believe that the earth and everything in it was divinely created by you O Lord, and I acknowledge that you are my creator.[110] I believe in the virgin birth of Jesus Christ,[111] I believe that he is fully God and fully man, I believe in his deity, his substitutionary atonement,

---

105 Galatians 3:14.
106 Psalm 37:22-26.
107 Matthew 6:25-30.
108 2 Corinthians 1:20.
109 John 15:26.
110 Genesis 1:1, 2:7, Psalm119:73.
111 Isaiah 7:14, Matthew 1:23.

his bodily resurrection,[112] and his soon physical return to earth,[113] and I believe he is fully God and fully man. I believe there is an eternal judgment for all souls living and dead,[114] and at the judgment, there is a literal heaven prepared for me and all those who believe in you, and a literal hell – lake of fire prepared for Satan and his demons and all who follow him.[115v] I believe that you – my Father, created me for a purpose and for a destiny, to declare your praises on this earth;[116] and by your power, I will achieve my destiny on this earth in the name of Jesus Christ.

I declare that, I will achieve my destiny and fulfill my purpose on this earth by your Spirit in the name of Jesus Christ. I declare that, as the salt of the earth, I will make it tolerable and will not lose my flavor; and I will impact my generation for Jesus. As the light of the world, I am a city set on a hill that cannot be hidden. My light shines bright, glowing in the dark for all to see. I will not hide my light but, let it shine brighter and brighter and my good deeds will glow for all to see as I impact other lives for Christ, so they will praise my heavenly Father.[117]

Father, as a vessel of your glory, I declare that I am an atmosphere changer. I declare the abundance of heaven to overflow in my life and home in the name of Jesus Christ. I declare over my finances and resources to align with heaven. I declare that the resources of heaven are being released unto me right now for the work of the ministry in the name of Jesus Christ. I declare over every impossible situation present in my life to reverse and align with the God of all possibilities in the name of Jesus Christ. I declare over every closed door that God has

---

112 Matthew 28:5-7.
113 Acts 1:11, Revelation 1:7.
114 Revelation 10:13, 11:18.
115 Revelation 19:20, 20:10-15.
116 1 Peter 2:9.
117 Matthew 5:13-15 (TLB).

opened for me to stay open right now, and every closed door God has closed, to stay closed in the name of Jesus Christ. I declare the purposes of God to manifest in my life in the name of Jesus Christ. I declare that the zeal of the house of the Lord is coming upon me right now, and as the deer pants after the water brooks, so I am panting after God. All my energy, strength, vigor, and passion for God that the enemy has compartmentalized and held captive, I command them to be released in the name of Jesus Christ. I thank you Lord for your Holy Spirit has caused these to manifest in my life in Jesus name, amen!

My Father, I hear your word, my eyes are open, my ears are open, and my heart is open, and I hear only your voice. I silent every other voice this day in the name of Jesus Christ. I choose to obey Your commands. I only hear and obey the voice of my Master – Jesus Christ of Nazareth because, I am his sheep. He knows me and I follow him as my shepherd. He has given unto me eternal life; and I shall never perish, neither shall any man pluck me out of his hand.[118] I choose to fill my mind with beauty and truth. I choose to meditate on all that is honorable, right, pure, lovely, good, virtuous, and praiseworthy.[119] I thank you my God, my King, my Lord, my Master, my good shepherd, and Your Majesty. I give you all the Praise, Glory, and Honor due unto You! And You alone, amen!

GREATNESS OF GOD

Who is like unto you my Lord? There is none that can compare to your greatness. None can stand before your Holiness. You are great and greatly to be praised. You sit upon the circle of the earth, and stretched out the heavens as a curtain. You spread them out as a tent to dwell

---

118 John 10:26-28.
119 Philippians 4:8.

in.[120] You sit upon your throne highly exalted. You made the heavens your throne and the earth your footstool.[121] Honor and Majesty are before you: strength and beauty are in your sanctuary. I give you all glory and strength due unto your Holy name.[122] Oh Lord my God, you are very great. There is nothing impossible with you my God, and there is no limitation in your presence. You are compassionate and gracious, abounding in love. You are clothe with Splendor and Majesty. You wrap yourself in light as with a garment. You make the clouds your chariot and ride on the wings of the wind. You make winds your messengers, and flames of fire your servants.[123] You Oh Lord are great, and greatly to be praised: you are to be feared above all gods.[124]

The Lord reigns in the heavens and in the earth. You Oh Lord are the creator and controller of the sky and the earth. The heavens declare your glory, and the firmament shows your handiwork. The earth is yours Oh Lord, and the fullness thereof; the world and all that dwells in it are equally yours. You founded the seas, and established it upon the floods.[125] Mighty Jehovah, you are robbed in Majesty, and armed with Strength. Your throne Oh Lord was established long ago, and you are from all eternity - O Eternal One. Ancient of Days, Jehovah is your name. Your garment is white as snow, and the hair of your head like pure wool. Your throne is like the fiery flame and your wheels as burning fire.[126] I worship you O Lord! You are Mighty! You are more powerful than the thunder of great waters and more powerful than the waves in the ocean - O Eternal on high.[127] There is none to compare to

---

120 Isaiah 40:22 (KJV).
121 Isaiah 66:1.
122 Psalm 96:6-7 (KJV).
123 Psalm 103:8, 104:1-4 (NIV).
124 Psalm 96:4 (KJV).
125 Psalm 19:1, 24:1, 2.
126 Daniel 7:9.
127 Psalm 93:1-4 (VOICE).

you. Every beast of the forest is yours; the cattle on a thousand hills are yours. The birds of the mountains and the wild beasts of the field are equally yours. The silver and gold belong to you my King and Lord of Hosts; and all souls are yours.[128]

Lord, you are the great God - The Eternal and great King, Supreme above all other gods.[129] EL Hakkabod – The God of Glory, your voice is upon many waters. The God of glory thunders. You Oh Lord thunders over the mighty waters. My Father, your voice Oh Lord is powerful. Elohim, your voice is full of Majesty.[130] O Eternal One, your majestic name is heard throughout the earth; your magnificent glory shines far above the skies. From the mouths and souls of infants and toddlers, the most innocent, you have decreed power to stop your adversaries and quash those who seek revenge.[131]

LORD OF ALL LORDS

Lord of the universe, you sit as King over all. You reign in your Splendor of Pomp and Majesty over your vast domain. Your brilliant light which radiates from your awesome presence fills the earth with your glory. I worship you in the Splendor of Your Holiness. Elohim, you sit enthroned as King over the flood and over the earth. You have dominion from sea to sea, and from the river unto the end of the earth.[132] You Oh Lord, rebuked the winds and the sea, and they obeyed your voice.[133] Elohim, you are enthroned as King forever and ever, amen! You have given me strength and blessed me with your peace – Shalom. Thank you my King and Lord of the universe. You are Lord over all the ele-

---

128 Psalm 50:10-12, Haggai 2:8.
129 Psalm 95:3.
130 Psalm 29:3-4 (NIV).
131 Psalm 8:1-2 (VOICE).
132 Psalm 72:8.
133 Matthew 8:26.

ments of nature - lightning and thunder, and over storm and flood. You are Lord over the storms of life. You are Lord over the trials and tribulations of life. You are Lord over sicknesses and diseases. You are Lord over any situation and circumstances of life. You are Lord of the valley and hills. I worship you my Lord of the universe; forever O Lord, your Word is settled in heaven.[134]

---

134 Psalm 119:89.

Write down your Testimony and Answers to Prayers

CHAPTER 2
Healing

Faith has to be tested to be faith. Untested faith is simply "motivational".

~ JOSEPHINE AKHAGBEME

THE BEGINNING OF THE STORY

THE DEVIL KNOWS AND UNDERSTANDS that we are limited by our humanity and senses of sight, hearing, touch, smell, taste, etc. He also uses the limited intellectual natural world to deceive a lot of people with the premise that, what cannot be tested and tried by experiment and observation is not accurate or true. The devil knows more than we do because; he operates in the unseen realm. He knows his limitations, and is aware of his imminent judgement and damnation. He knows that he lost the battle over humanity on the cross of Calvary and subsequently, he is aware of his defeat by Jesus Christ. Additionally, he knows that Christians have the power and authority of God Almighty to cause adverse damage to his wicked kingdom. Unfortunately, many Christians are not aware of whose and who they are in Christ. They are not aware of the tremendous power and authority to trample upon the enemy's destructive agenda triumphantly. Sadly, Christians are not utilizing their authority in Jesus Christ as they ought. Satan's goal is to keep the body of believers from this awareness and stop them from utilizing their authority to pull down his kingdom.

God created the unseen realm and His name is El Roi – The God who sees.[135] He created this unseen realm, and He is Lord over that realm; and he is telling us to trust Him. The devil came to steal, kill, and destroy; this is the beginning of the story. He has the tools and people to carry out his destructive agenda against God. The devil starts and ends in the beginning of the story, and he wants us to be stuck there with him. This people, is not the end of the victorious story. No one writes a story with a beginning that does not have an end. No one gets a complete story from the beginning. A compelling story has a beginning and an end. The good news is this: the end of the story was written by Jesus Christ Himself and it is victorious. The final story was written and accomplished when Jesus Christ came, died, and rose again from the dead. By accomplishing his mission on earth, he established for us, victorious strategy to overcome the evil one and his lies.

The scripture says that the devil was a murderer from the beginning, and cannot tolerate truth because; he is void of anything that contains truth. At the core of his character, he is a liar; everything he speaks originates in these lies because he is the father of lies.[136] The entire enemy's mission is a LIE. In a synopsis, every evil we see on earth and experience in our lives, that does not align with the truth of God's word are all lies; and there is no iota of truth in it. The pain, heartaches, brokenness, sickness, diseases, disappointments, addictions, hopelessness, suicide, wickedness, murder, etc. are all lies, though very real. Don't get me wrong; I am not discounting the real experiences and pain of anyone, neither am I in denial however; I call these FACTS. I acknowledge the realness of human depravity in sufferings and pains, and God is still using science and medicine to heal and restore health today.

---

135 Genesis 16:13.
136 John 8:43-45.

He chooses the means to heal his children and he can do it whichever way he pleases. The truth is that, God created science as well as all inventions for the good of humanity and for His glory.

In speaking about *the relationship between the human nature and behavior (psychology) - which utilizes reasoning and the observation of nature as its primary source; and the exploration of God and His world (theology) - which utilizes God's Word, both are subject to God's sovereignty and serve His ends* (Entwistle, 2010, p. 148).[vi] Additionally, God integrates all these disciplines and knowledge for the betterment of humanity "And we know that all things work together for good to them that love God, to them who are the called according to his purpose."[137]

FACTS AND TRUTH

There is a huge difference between FACTS and TRUTH. The fact of a matter does not equate to the truth. FACT as defined by Merriam-Webster Collegiate dictionary is: the quality of being actual; something that truly exists or happens; something that has actual existence; a true piece of information. It further defines TRUTH as: the quality or state of being true; sincerity in action, character, and utterance.

The Bible talks about what TRUTH really means. Note the different scriptures below in the KJV:

> "Thy word is true from the beginning: and every one of thy righteous judgments endureth forever" Psalm 119:160.
>
> "Sanctify them through thy truth: thy word is truth" John 17:16.
>
> "Lead me in thy truth, and teach me: for thou art the God of my salvation; on thee do I wait all the day" Psalm 25:5.

---

[137] Romans 8:28 (KJV).

"The elder unto the elect lady and her children, whom I love in the truth; and not I only, but also all they that have known the truth; For the truth's sake, which dwelleth in us, and shall be with us forever. Grace be with you, mercy, and peace, from God the Father, and from the Lord Jesus Christ, the Son of the Father, in truth and love" 2 John 1-3.

"This is he that came by water and blood, even Jesus Christ; not by water only, but by water and blood. And it is the Spirit that beareth witness, because the Spirit is truth" 1 John 5:6.

Truth cannot exist without God; just like a created world cannot exist without a Creator; or can peace exist without the Prince of Peace – Jesus Christ.[138] I am not going into an argument of subjective or objective truth. The Word of God is God Himself and does not need proof "In the beginning was the Word, and the Word was with God, and the Word was God. The same was in the beginning with God. All things were made by him; and without him was not anything made that was made."[139]

TRUTH endures forever in contrast to the changing nature of FACTS. Facts are limited by the finite nature and reality of our world and human flawed view of it. The opposite of Truth is Lie. The only way to overcome lies is to counter it with truth. When the enemy tells you that: the bad things from your past cannot be forgiven, or you are not valuable, no one loves you, you are ugly, you are a loser, you are sick, you are dumb, you are foolish, or you are worthless, etc. these are all lies, and what you entertain or allow into your life becomes the truth. The enemy thrives when you believe his lies. God, through Jesus Christ gave us His word in overcoming the world and the evil one.

---

138 Isaiah 9:6.
139 1 John 1:1-3 (KJV).

You may ask: why are words so important? And why is it a big deal? The truth is that God spoke this earthly realm and everything we see into manifestation by His spoken Word.[140] He communicates to us with words. The enemy constantly bombard human minds with evil thoughts that are contrary to God's word; and if allowed to dwell in the heart and spoken out audibly, he uses them to bind and oppress. Every thought the enemy suggest to the mind is a lie, and these lies if allowed, gives him the legal ground to oppress people. Words are so important because, it is the medium with which things are spoken into manifestation in our earthly realm. You can either speak into manifestation what God says or the lies of the enemy. Jesus confirms the efficacy and power of truth in God's word when he spoke to His Father and said "my prayer is for you not to take them out of the world, but to protect them from the evil one. They are not of the world, even as I am not of the world. Sanctify them by the truth: thy word is truth."[141] The bible actually clearly states that; TRUTH is God's word.

Having briefly differentiated what FACTS and TRUTH is; it is no surprise that the devil uses the FACTS to camouflage and operate. I stated above, anything that does not align or agree with the word of God is not true but a lie. For instance, sickness and disease may exist as a fact in someone's life but, that is just the beginning of the story. However, the truth of the matter which supersedes the fact, is the end of the story and this perfectly aligns in agreement with what Jesus came to accomplish for all believers which is – healing, restoration, deliverance, liberty, justice, peace, joy, hope, eternity with God, etc. The truth always sets you free.[142] You have to embrace truth – truth of God's word which acknowledges that you are beloved; you are free; and you are forgiven.

---

140 Genesis 1, Psalm 90:2, Isaiah 45:18, John 1:1-3.
141 John 17:13-17.
142 John 8:33.

In speaking about the final story – the end of the story, which was accomplished on the cross of Calvary when Jesus paid the price for TRUTH, the scripture says about Jesus Christ: He is despised and rejected of men; a man of sorrows, and acquainted with grief: and we hid as it were our faces from him; he was despised, and we esteemed him not. Surely he hath borne our griefs, and carried our sorrows: yet we did esteem him stricken, smitten of God, and afflicted. But he was wounded for our transgressions; he was bruised for our iniquities: the chastisement of our peace was upon him; and with his stripes we are healed. All we like sheep have gone astray; we have turned everyone to his own way; and the Lord hath laid on him the iniquity of us all.[143]

THE ENEMY'S WRONG LABEL

Jesus Christ had to suffer hurt, pain, injuries, rejection, shame, disappointment, loneliness, sorrow, suffering, affliction, punishment, oppression, opposition, was despised, stricken, and crushed for our sake, in order to bring us healing, wholeness, and peace. Beloved, we have to look away from all that easily distract us and focus our eyes on Jesus, who is the Author and Perfecter of our faith, who for the joy of accomplishing the goal set before Him endured the cross, disregarding the shame, and sat down at the right hand of the throne of God; revealing His deity, His authority, and the completion of His work.[144] This beloved, is the end of the story that the enemy is trying to keep from us. He wants to keep us in the beginning of the story rather than to progress and operate from the end of the story.

In other words, sicknesses, diseases, death (separation from earth), pain, hunger, heartbreaks, disappointments, wars, abuses, divorces, poverty, racism, tribalism, injustice, etc. are all the beginning of the

---
143 Isaiah 53:4-6.
144 Hebrews 12:2 (AMP).

story, but not the end of the story, hallelujah! The devil thinks he is in control but the end of the story which is the hope we have as Christians is that, God is still redeeming today. He says that, the threshing floors will be covered in grain; the vats will spill over with new wine and fresh oil. He will compensate you for the years that the locusts have eaten—the swarming locusts, his great army that he unleashed against you. *In that day,* you will eat plenty *of food* and always have enough, so you will praise His name, The Eternal One, your God who is merciful to you. Never again will His people be shamed *among the nations.*[145]

There is no conclusion to a story from the beginning. The entirety of a story is not in the beginning. The end of a story is where the truth lies. Recently (August 2016), I went out with a friend to get ice tea. On our way home, as I reached out to take a sip, I noticed a little sticker on the cup with the words "diet coke". I thought they got our order wrong and may have given us someone else's order. We decided to turn around and get our correct order. Our decision to go back to the restaurant was based on the sticker on the cup. At this time, we had not tasted what was inside the cup. As we made the turn, I decided to take a sip and have a taste of the diet coke. To my surprise, it was not a diet coke as the sticker states rather, it was the iced tea we ordered. The liquid inside the cup was the correct drink but it was mislabeled.

The devil operates so much like the sticker on the cup. He puts a wrong label on an individual contrary to what God has deposited inside that person. The sticker is deceptive and misleading. This deceptive nature and tactics of the evil one may sometimes cause delay or loss. God has blessed his children and by "his divine power, has given us everything we need for a godly life through our knowledge of him who called us by his own glory and goodness."[146] Because humans are limited in their finite minds, and mostly focused on the

---
145 Joel 2:26-16 (VOICE).
146 2 Peter 1:3 (NIV).

factual physicality of life, they tend not to concentrate on what God says but rather be limited by what they see. The sticker on my cup was a lie. It was a deception from the reality of the iced tea inside my cup. It took me an intentional proactive step to discover the truth. The devil usually corrupts the truth of God's word. For instance, if God says you are blessed, the enemy's sticker says you are cursed. If God says you are healed, the enemy's sticker says you are sick and there is no cure. If God says you are beloved, the enemy's sticker says you are unwanted and unloved, etc. What label has the enemy stamped on you? What is the sticker of your life saying? What lies are you believing?

THE LIES OF SATAN

Satan and his demons operate in the beginning of the story of fallen man and nature, and he ends there. This is a lie and it is a wrong label. Satan and his demons try to convince us that the beginning is the end of the story. A lot of people bought into the lie of Satan and that is why they do not see results or answers to their prayers. Once you get this truth in your spirit, you will begin to experience all that Jesus Christ manifested on the cross of Calvary – and this is where the end of the story begins and end. You will begin to understand that, the enemy uses your body to lie to you through sicknesses, diseases, pains, tiredness, fatigue, depression, anxiety, hopelessness, etc.; he uses the doctors to lie to you with their diagnosis based on the limited FACTS they possess; he uses your senses to lie to you through what you feel, see, taste, touch, etc.; he uses the news on television of the hopelessness around the world to lie to you; he uses all the physicality of humanity to lie to you with all that is factual to human senses; and these are all based on the flawed and fallen nature of humanity. I am here to tell you that all these are lies and not the truth.

Sicknesses, diseases, and all the depravity of humanity is a curse.[147] While healing is a promise, curse is the result of disobedience to God's commandments.[148] In order to break the curses that came upon humanity due to this disobedience and release us from its consequences, Jesus had to come to earth to be born, died, and rose again.[149] Only those that are Christians have access to these blessings. The benefits of the kingdom of God are for the children of the kingdom. Therefore, as believers, we can receive all that Jesus Christ came to accomplish on the cross of Calvary through the Holy Spirit for:

> Christ redeemed us from that self-defeating, cursed life by absorbing it completely into himself. Do you remember the Scripture that says, "Cursed is everyone who hangs on a tree"? That is what happened when Jesus was nailed to the cross: He became a curse, and at the same time dissolved the curse. And now, because of that, the air is cleared and we can see that Abraham's blessing is present and available for non-Jews, too. We are *all* able to receive God's life, his Spirit, in and with us by believing—just the way Abraham received it. In Christ's family, there can be no division into Jew and non-Jew, slave and free, male and female. Among us you are all equal. That is, we are all in a common relationship with Jesus Christ. Also, since you are Christ's family, then you are Abraham's famous "descendant," heirs according to the covenant promises.[150]

In order to experience the supernatural power of God in your life; and healing and wholeness, you have to go beyond what you see and feel and

---

147 Genesis 3.
148 Deuteronomy 11:26-28.
149 1 John 3:7-9.
150 Galatians 3:13-14, 29 (MSG).

instead, dwell on and believe the truth of God's Word in all aspects of your life, and with the understanding that all he has promised, already exist. For you to believe the truth of God's word, you have to know it and be aware that it exists. For you to know it, you have to read about it: "But how are men to call upon him in whom they have not believed? And how are they to believe in him of whom they have never heard? And how are they to hear without a preacher? And how can men preach unless they are sent? As it is written, "How beautiful are the feet of those who preach good news!" But they have not all obeyed the gospel; for Isaiah says, "Lord, who has believed what he has heard from us?""" [151] This truth cannot be head knowledge residing on your intellectual mind; it has to go deep into your heart, and you will have to agree and align with it in order for it to manifest in your life and produce results. "Take to heart this advice: Do your best to present yourself to God as one approved, a worker who does not need to be ashamed and who correctly handles the word of truth."[152]

The end of the story was written when Jesus Christ died and rose again. He wrote the victorious end of the story with his precious blood and this cannot be erased – it is permanent and no one can change it. Jesus Christ was slain for all mankind in order to manifest victory for us; "worthy is the Lamb, who was slain to receive power and wealth and wisdom and strength and honor and glory and praise!"[153] The only way we can experience the truth of God's word is through faith and belief. You must believe in your heart that, all the physical experiences of life are FACTS and not the final TRUTH and then, counter it with the truth of God's word - the Bible. Remember, anything that does not align with the Word of God is a lie. You have to constantly and ceaselessly speak the truth of God's word over your body, your mind,

---

151 Romans 10:14-16 (RSV).
152 2 Timothy 2:15 (NIV).
153 Revelation 5:12 (KJV).

your situation, your circumstances, your pain, etc. and eventually, the truth of God's word will prevail and you will experience the end of the story – the finished victorious work of Calvary in your life.

THE FINISHED WORK OF THE CROSS

THE END OF THE STORY

The end of the story was noted in the bible when Jesus Christ was nailed to that cross of Calvary, before he took his final breath, he declared "it is finished."[154] At this point, there was a closure to the end of the story with those words. The line of completion was drawn. Jesus Christ paid the ultimate and final price for our healing. No other price is left to be paid by anyone else forever "knowing that you were not redeemed with corruptible things, *like* silver or gold, from your aimless conduct *received* by tradition from your fathers, but with the precious blood of Christ, as of a lamb without blemish and without spot. He indeed was foreordained before the foundation of the world, but was manifest in these last times for you who through Him believe in God, who raised Him from the dead and gave Him glory, so that your faith and hope are in God."[155] We just have to accept, believe, and receive the finished work with thanksgiving; it is a free gift to us from God Almighty, and it is yours right now if you can only ask.

The finished work of Calvary which is the end of the story was established when Jesus rose from the dead and declared "all power in heaven and earth has been given to me."[156] The result of this finished work include: no one can curse whom God has not cursed, or denounce

---

154 John 19:30.
155 1 Peter 1:18-21 (NKJV).
156 Matthew 28:18-20.

whom God has not denounced;[157] no undeserved curse for any reason will come upon you;[158] if we walk in the light, as he is in the light, we have fellowship with one another, and the blood of Jesus, his Son, purifies us from all sin;[159] we are forgiven and set free; for whom the Son sets free, is free indeed;[160] we do not have our own righteousness, but that which is through the faith of Christ, the righteousness which is of God by faith;[161] I am the righteousness of God in Christ Jesus.

SHAME AND GUILT OF OUR PAST

The devil cannot bring guilt of our past in order to hinder our healing. We must watch out for this lie of the devil who usually whispers that, your past sins are the cause of your present situation and pain. This is a lie from the pit of hell. When you ask Christ to forgive your sins, he does just that. Before we ever had a past, Jesus died on the cross and paid the price. We could not help ourselves, and that is why he came, "For scarcely for a righteous man will one die; yet perhaps for a good man someone would even dare to die. But God demonstrates His own love toward us, in that while we were still sinners, Christ died for us. Much more then, having now been justified by His blood, we shall be saved from wrath through Him."[162]

The devil uses the shame of our past as a tool to control our lives. This can keep you from receiving the free gift of salvation, deliverance, and liberty you need in order to progress into a higher and deeper relationship with God, and a meaningful life experiences with others.

---

157 Numbers 23:8.
158 Proverbs 26:2.
159 1 John 1:7.
160 John 8:36.
161 Philippians 3:9.
162 Romans 5:7-9 (NKJV).

Everyone has a past and nobody is perfect otherwise, I will not be qualified to write this book; "all have sinned, and come short of the glory of God."[163] If you allow what has happened in your life to keep you bound from receiving your freedom, you will continue to have a victim mentality; which houses an orphan spirit of rejection, anger, unworthiness, unloved, regrets, self-pity, and unforgiveness.

Our past is covered by the blood of Christ. We are brand new, we are holy, we are spotless because of Jesus Christ "For as the heaven is high above the earth, so great is his mercy toward them that fear him. As far as the east is from the west, so far hath he removed our transgressions from us. As a father pitieth his children, so the Lord pitieth them that fear him.[164] There is no sin that can shock God; there is no sin that will take him by surprise; and there is no sin that he will not forgive. If we come to him in true repentance, and confess our sins before him, he is faithful and just to forgive us our sins, and to cleanse us from all unrighteousness.[165]

You cannot continue to live in the shame of your past. Jesus Christ have washed our past and its shame away with His blood but if you confess your sins, God will pardon, forgive and restore you. "THEREFORE, [there is] now no condemnation (no adjudging guilty of wrong) for those who are in Christ Jesus, who live [and] walk not after the dictates of the flesh, but after the dictates of the Spirit. For the law of the Spirit of life [which is] in Christ Jesus [the law of our new being] has freed me from the law of sin and of death".[166]

When the devil comes to you with condemnation from your past, remind him of his imminent future in the lake of fire for all eternity, "And the devil that deceived them was cast into the lake of fire

---

163 Romans 3:23 (KJV).
164 Psalm 103:11-13 (KJV).
165 1 John 1:9 (KJV).
166 Romans 8:1-2 (AMP).

and brimstone, where the beast and the false prophet are, and shall be tormented day and night for ever and ever."[167] It is so important that Christians should live right and pray in the spirit on all occasions. "But God's truth stands firm like a great rock, and nothing can shake it. It is a foundation stone with these words written on it: "The Lord knows those who are really his," and "A person who calls himself a Christian should not be doing things that are wrong."[168]

THE GOOD NEWS OF THE GOSPEL

The healing we desire, and the breakthrough we've been waiting for, are all concluded and settled forever on that cross of Calvary "it is finished". We are healed, we are delivered, and we are free. For this purpose, the Son of God was made manifest in order to destroy the works of the devil.[169] Jesus Christ came and declared: The spirit of the Lord is upon me, because he has anointed me to proclaim the good news (of the gospel) to the poor. This good news is: freedom, peace, restoration, deliverance, healing, liberty, the revelation of the messiah – The Risen Christ, Jesus;[170] and Eternity with Christ in heaven. Beloved, this is the victorious end of the story – the good news of the gospel.

Jesus himself said, he saw Satan fall from heaven. His fall was so fast and swift, a bolt of lightning from the sky. His defeat was also as swift as his fall from heaven, in lightning speed.[171] Knowing this, Satan and his demons are operating from a defeated platform of damnation. He is also operating from the beginning of the story of the fall of humanity. The truth is that we as believers, are operating from the end

---

167 Revelation 20:10 (KJV).
168 2 Timothy 2:19 (TLB).
169 1 John 3:8.
170 Luke 4:18-19.
171 Luke 10:18.

of the story of the victory of the resurrection of Jesus Christ. We are operating from a higher dimension of the supernatural with signs and wonders following. We are operating from a higher domain of authority of the name of Jesus Christ. And God has raised us up with Christ and seated us with him in the heavenly realms in Christ Jesus.[172] When this truth of Satan's defeat and overcoming victory of believers was revealed, Jesus, full of joy through the Holy Spirit, said, "I praise you, Father, Lord of heaven and earth, because you have hidden these things from the wise and learned, and revealed them to little children. Yes, Father, for this was your good pleasure."[173]

Beloved, this is the good news of the end of the story that has been revealed to us and we ought to start operating from this platform of authority knowing that, through Jesus Christ, we have overcome in the power of the Holy Spirit. We ought to start declaring as priests of the Most High; for when you delight in the Almighty, and lift up your face to God in prayer, He will hear you, and you will pay your vows. You will also declare a thing, and it will be established for you; so, light will shine on your ways.[174]

Believe — a Major Key to Healing

Jesus Christ, through His Holy Spirit is still healing today; and he is the same yesterday, today, and forever,[175] he will never change, hallelujah! The same Jesus, who healed when he walked the streets of this earth,[176] is the same Jesus who is still healing today and will continue forever. The same virtue he operated in during his earthly ministry is present

---

172 Ephesians 2:6.
173 Luke 10:21 (NIV).
174 Job 22:26-28 (NKJV).
175 Hebrews 13:8.
176 Matthew 10:1.

today through the power of the Holy Spirit. He has sent us into the entire world to preach the gospel to everyone. He promised us that, these signs shall follow us that believe; in my name (Jesus Christ), shall they (believers) cast out devils; they (believers) shall speak with new tongues; they (believers) shall take up serpents; and if they (believers) drink any deadly thing, it shall not hurt them (believers); they (believers) shall lay hands on the sick, and the sick shall recover.[177] The end of the story is – victory, deliverance, healing, peace, hope, joy, restoration, liberty, eternity with Jesus Christ, etc.

A lot of Christians today, including theological students who are being trained in bible schools do not believe in healing and deliverance. The truth of the matter is that; you cannot experience anything you do not believe. These individuals may have the Holy Spirit in them through salvation however, because of their unbelief in these specific areas of healing and deliverance, they have suppressed the Holy Spirit in demonstrating his miraculous power in their lives and ministry with signs and wonders following. "Jesus Christ did not bother to work wondrous miracles in Nazareth because the people did not believe."[178] Do you wonder why a lot of preachers do not believe that miracles are still present in our generation today? Do you wonder if this is due to their unbelief and the fact that they have never experienced a personal miraculous touch of God in their lives? The power of a personal touch from God is what such people need in order for them to believe. Therefore, belief is very important in obtaining your healing; and it is one of the element utilized in God's kingdom to access his provision.

God is supernatural and desires to display his supernatural power in our lives. We do not have the authority to dictate to the Holy Spirit what he ought to perform and not perform. We cannot compartmentalize the Holy Spirit with our flawed myopic and finite minds. Signs

---

[177] Mark 16:15-20.
[178] Matthew 13:57-58 (VOICE).

and wonders ought to characterize the lives of all believers because, our God is a supernatural God who reveals his power in signs and wonders. God is limitless but humans limit him in their lives and ministries from displaying his power through unbelief. If you allow him in freedom, you will experience that part of his supernatural with signs and wonders following. Below is one of my many healing stories. I have experienced healing personally from paralysis, migraine, and lump in my breast.

My Healing Story

The enemy attempted to convince me to accept the beginning of the story when on July 30, 2012; I woke up with this sudden eye disease. I went to have my eyes checked on August 20, 2012; and it was so severe, that I had to visit the emergency room on September 1, 2012. After the exams, I was diagnosed with Binocular Diplopia disease, which may require using special glasses with built-in-prisms, or surgery on the muscles of the eye. The symptoms in my body included: double vision, cross-eyed, dizziness, and tongue-numbness, weird taste in my tongue, mild headache, tiredness, lazy eyes, and sleepiness. Every time I would walk, it felt like I was stepping into a ditch. Any time I looked at my kids from one direction, they would tell me that my eyes were looking at them from a different direction. I had an MRA/MRV done, and other special tests, in addition to visiting an oral surgeon, Neuro Ophthalmology, Neuro Oncologist, a Neurologist, and a Radiologist.

My Neurologist referred me for surgery as a last attempt to locate the cause of my eye disease. This last surgery was required in order to extract fluid from my spine, for a final determination regarding my treatment. On September 19, 2012, after the visit with my Neurologist, and as I sat in my car waiting to complete the test I was referred to, I heard the Lord spoke to my spirit that I will testify about this disease because; he is going to heal me. I immediately asked one thing from the

Lord which was, for him to give me a testimony and a song from this experience. After speaking with my friend Nkechi Ekezie a day before my surgery, she advised against the surgery, and for me to believe God all the way for my healing. Prior to this time, my husband had been in prayer with me for healing based on the finished work of the cross, and was opposed to the surgery as well. This was the confirmation I needed. I immediately went ahead to cancel my appointment, and put my trust in God for my total healing with the understanding that, the doctors were unable to help me.

Afterwards, I decided to pursue my recovering and intervention spiritually because; the doctors could not locate the cause of this disease in my body medically. I proceeded on researching all the detailed parts of eye and brain connection, and wrote the names out. I saturated myself with the word of God and constantly declared the truth of God's word over my eyes, and all the specific parts of my eye and brain connection. I wrote down several healing scriptures that I declared all day long. I read the healing book written by Kenneth E. Hagin titled: Healing Scriptures. This is a very good book with lots of healing scriptures. I wrote down scriptures all over my bathroom mirror. Anytime I looked at the mirror, I would hear the voice of the devil, mocking me saying "I will never get well". I would hear him whispering to my ears that I still have the symptoms and my prayers are not working.

My husband prayed and anointed me with oil several times. Anytime I drove my car, I would patch one eye (like a pirate) to relieve the symptoms. At work, one of my co-workers told me that, she had similar problem and the only solution was to have surgery and wear a special glass my entire life time. These are the voices of hopelessness and faithlessness I encountered. I decided to stop talking to this particular co-worker about my decision because; I did not want to surround myself with negative people who do not share my optimistic view for healing.

During that period, I knew that my only hope depends on God as my healer and not on the doctors who do not have a solution for me. I rested my entire hope and trust in the word of God regarding my healing. I believed with my whole heart that God still heals today, and I was determined to trust him all the way. The symptoms continued for about seven months. Throughout, I saturated myself with healing scriptures and the word of God. Confessing and declaring the finished work of healing over my eyes with thanksgiving. Sure enough, faith started rising up within my spirit. Anytime the enemy would suggest negative hopeless thoughts to my spirit, I would counter it with the word of God.

On the seventh month, I was sitting down one beautiful afternoon, and as I turned to speak to my husband Bon, I realized in that instant, I did not experience any symptoms. At first, I was not sure, but turned my head again the second time just to be very sure. I started screaming with joy and thanksgiving jumping up and down. At that moment, I realized that I was miraculously healed. The way the disease came upon me suddenly, was the same way it left my body suddenly. I realized that the first day I prayed and asked God for my healing, he heard my prayers; "They shall not labour in vain, nor bring forth for trouble; for they are the seed of the blessed of the Lord, and their offspring with them. And it shall come to pass, that before they call, I will answer; and while they are yet speaking, I will hear.[179]

It took seven months for my healing to manifest. Some people's healing manifest instantly; some are healed through medical process; for some, it takes months like in my situation; for some it takes years; and yet for some, they will not experience their healing on this side of our earthly realm. Regardless of the situation you may find yourself, realize that "all things work together for good to them that love God,

---

179 Isaiah 65:23-24 (KJV).

to them who are called according to his purpose."[180] Understand that it is God Almighty who determines our healing. All that is required of us is to trust him, believe all that he has spoken, and ask for the grace to accept his will for our lives in all situation. It is of our Father's good pleasure to give us of the kingdom.[181] All that exist in God's kingdom includes: healing, liberty, deliverance, blessings, righteousness, peace, and joy in the Holy Ghost.[182] The Lord not only completely healed me but gave me powerful anointed healing songs that produced more healing miracles as I sing them.

Faith in Prayer

Jesus came in the power of the Holy Spirit to heal broken hearts, set captives free, loose chains of bondage from the lives of people, open blind yes, and restored spiritual awareness of the authority we possess as Christians, to set at liberty those who are bound, and declare that the year of the Lord is here.[183] The authority to stop the destructive agenda of Satan and his demons, have been given to us as believers in overcoming all satanic oppressions; and nothing by any means will injure or harm us.[184] Therefore, we must not accept anything less than what Christ established on the cross of Calvary.

Faith, putting it simply, is when you are aware and have a settled belief that what God says in his word concerning your situation is true and it exist already without any doubt. And based on that knowledge and awareness, what you are asking God to do for you is not from what does not exist but rather, from what is in existence already. Faith

---

180 Romans 8:28 (KJV).
181 Luke 12:32.
182 Romans 14:16-18.
183 Luke 4:18-19.
184 Luke 10:19.

believes God more than anything or anyone else. In other words, you are willing and ready in your heart to receive what God has promised and concluded in His Word, way before you see it.

This passage gives us further insight to what faith is all about "Without faith it is impossible to please God, because anyone who comes to him must believe that he exists and that he rewards those who earnestly seek him."[185] The Greek word for **"earnestly"** in this verse is *ekzēteō* which means: to seek out, be held responsible for, search intently with the greatest care.[vii] The responsibility to earnestly seek out with a deliberate intention for your healing and anything else in the kingdom of God, rest on the individual that believes. The individual has to have a desire in their heart in order to receive.

The Greek word for **"faith"** in the passage above is *pistis* which means: faithfulness, proof, belief, trust, with an implication that actions based on that trust may follow. This faith often refers to the Christian system of belief and lifestyle.[viii] Faith therefore, ought to be accompanied by action. Faith is the proof of your belief and trust in God for what He has spoken and accomplished already, which truly exist and is available for you.

It is this same faith (*pistis*), that these men possessed and exhibited in action: Abel (who offered God a better sacrifice), Enoch (was taken from this life), Noah (was warned and he obeyed God), Abraham (obeyed God when called to go to a foreign land), Isaac (blessed Jacob and Esau), Jacob (when he was dying blessed his grandchildren), Joseph (on his dead bed gave further instructions for children of Israel and regarding his burial), Moses (his parents hid him because they had a glimpse of his great future), Moses (as an adult refused to be linked to an ungodly lineage), etc. (reference Hebrews 11). All these great men of the bible possess one common attribute – action. They heard from

---

185 Hebrews 11:6 (NIV).

God, believed Him, followed through with action, and put their trust in God for the outcome.

God is not asking you to exercise what has never been done. Looking at the list above, these great men of the bible had no other way to experience God and fulfill the mandate and purpose they were created for, except by faith. Everything in the kingdom of God is by faith. Faith therefore, is coming to a place of knowing, of full realization, and of total awareness that what you have asked for has already been given way before your need became evident to you. Your belief and faith has to be based on God's Word, because God stands by His Word to perform it. Faith is also personal because "the just shall live by his faith."[186]

On earth, we need currency - a form of tender as a medium of exchange to purchase goods and services. This currency is already established and exist in order to be utilized. Similarly, heaven require a form of spiritual tender to access and obtain what exist there already. Heaven's tender is FAITH. In other words, the tender you need to fulfil your purpose and destiny on this earth, and to get what you desire (healing, salvation, deliverance, wealth, peace, joy, etc.) is through the medium of FAITH. Your faith in God is attached to the end result of your desire. You cannot separate faith from the result, for without faith it is impossible to please God.

God had faith when He created the earth. It was His faith in action when He spoke, "Let there be!"[187] Faith is knowing and having a settlement in your spirit, a proof and assurance that what you have asked God for, believed God for, and hoped in God for has already happened. You can actually see the outcome – the finished work of Calvary in your spirit. In alignment with your actions, attitude, and confessions, you can turn God's promises into performances simply by putting your faith into action. Faith is linked to God and both cannot be separated.

---

186 Habakkuk 2:4 (KJV).
187 Genesis 1:3.

All you need is in God and to access it, you must believe that God exist, and he rewards those who diligently seek him.

Faith is the spiritual atmosphere you want to entertain when you ask God for healing; and sometimes, God's will may not be to heal in all cases but, "the prayer of faith shall save the sick, and the Lord shall raise him up; and if he have committed sins, they shall be forgiven him."[188] In speaking about the prayer of faith and the gift of healing, the King James Study Bible Commentary noted:

> *God does not always choose to heal, He sometimes does. When a Christian is sick, he should confess his known sins, and God may heal him if the sickness is caused by sin. He may also be led to ask his elders to anoint him, with oil and pray for his healing. Some diseases experienced by Christians could be prevented by trusting God as Yahweh – Rapha, and allowing Him to deal with those things in their lives causing stress, anger, and worry. The prayer of faith does not include a gift of healing. It does not exert extraordinary Spiritual strength[189] otherwise; all Spiritual Christians would be healthy;[190] nor does it merely involve the ritual of calling the elders of the church to pray and anoint the individual with oil. The prayer of faith discerns God's will and perseveres until it is accomplished. God's will, however, is not to heal in every case, and true faith can discern and accept that."*[191][lix]

Jesus Christ has the solution for ALL the problems that we as humans will ever encounter in this life, but we have to access the solution in faith. Way before you got sick, there was a provision of healing already put in place "who his own self bare our sins in his own body on the

---

188 James 5:15 (KJV).
189 Acts 3:12,16.
190 3 John 2.
191 Romans 8:26-27.

tree, that we, being dead to sins, should live unto righteousness: by whose stripes ye were healed."[192] If you know and realize this, claim your healing based on that revealed Word regarding the healing you need because, He is your Jehovah Rapha. Once you grasp this truth, start thanking Him for the provision of healing. Now you know the truth which is the solution, and the truth of His Word have set you free. God's Word is our inheritance. We have to actually read it, believe it, and allow the Holy Spirit to illuminate its truth in our hearts in order to produce all that we need to live a healthy and godly life here on earth.

On September 29th, 2009, I had this terrible migraine headache all day, and was frustrated and tired of it. I later went into my closet, which was my prayer spot where I usually had my quiet time in prayer and reading God's Word. I asked the Lord in prayer to take away the headache and heal me based on His Word in Isaiah 53:3-5. As I was reading that chapter, I told the Lord that I do not only want healing, but I also want a healing song as well. Shortly after, the Lord gave me this healing song which I sang for a long time over and over. Praise God, I was healed completely singing the song over me. The Lord revealed Himself to me through His name of Jehovah Rapha which means: The Lord our healer.[193] The words to the song goes like this:

> *He was despised and rejected of men*
> *A man of sorrows acquainted with grief*
> *Jesus he bore all my griefs*
> *Jesus he carried my sorrows*
> *He was stricken, smitten and afflicted of God*
> *And he carried my sin upon the cross*
> *I am healed by his wounds*

---
192 1 Peter 2:24.
193 Exodus 15:26.

I am healed with his stripes
I am healed in the name of Jesus Christ
I am healed by his wounds
I am healed with his stripes
I am healed in the name of the Lord[x]

As noted in my introduction, the Lord told me, He will teach me how to pray His Word that will produce results. Since then, I have been praying God's word over every situation and circumstances I encounter in my life and spiritual walk. God is bound by His word;[194] and watches over His word to perform it,[195] according to his will for us. When you put your trust, and hope in the miraculous and supernatural God, and delight yourself in the Lord, he will give you the desires of your heart. When you commit your way to Him, he will bring to pass all he has promised.[196] Healing (emotional or physical) is part of his promises for his children. Those who have regard for the weak are blessed. The Lord will deliver them in times of trouble. The Lord will protect and preserve them. They are blessed in the land, and He will not allow their enemies to triumph over them. The Lord will sustain them on their sickbed and restore health to them from their bed of illness.[197]

Jesus is inviting you, "Come to Me, all *you* who labor and are heavy laden, and I will give you rest. Take My yoke upon you and learn from Me, for I am gentle and lowly in heart, and you will find rest for your souls.[198] The Eternal One is saying to you: "If you are thirsty, come here; come, there's water for all. Whoever is poor and penniless can still come and buy the food I sell. There's no cost—here, have

---

194 Jeremiah 1:12.
195 Ezekiel 12:25.
196 Psalm 27:4-6.
197 Psalm 41:1-3.
198 Matthew 11:28-19 (NKJV).

some food, *hearty and delicious,* and beverages, *pure and good.* I don't understand why you spend your money for things that don't nourish or work so hard for what leaves you empty. Attend to Me and eat what is good; enjoy the richest, *most delectable* of things. Listen closely, and come *even* closer. My words will give life, for I will make a covenant with you that cannot be broken, *a promise* Of My enduring *presence* and support like I gave to David."[199] Are you willing to cast all upon Him? Are you willing to dare to trust him? Are you willing to believe Him for your healing? Are you willing to receive what he has to offer? It is only those who believe that will be able to partake of this free gift.

HEALING PRAYER

Now, begin to pray this prayer in faith and belief

My Father, I come to you in repentance. I humble myself under your mighty hand.[200] I repent of my sins of (name sin) that will hinder my healing. I forgive (name individual) who has hurt me through (name hurt). Empower me by your Spirit to totally forgive (name individual), and in addition, I forgive myself also. I denounce every involvement with the works of darkness. I open my heart to you my God, to do what you want with me. I thank you for hearing me. I believe I am your beloved child. I believe you desire to heal and restore health to my body.[201] I believe healing is for your children[202] and as such, it is for me. I believe you want to heal me because you love me so dearly, and as a

---

199 Isaiah 55:1-3 (VOICE).
200 1 Peter 5:6.
201 1 John 1:2.
202 Matthew 15:24-28.

good Father, you give good gifts to your children.[203] My Father, I pray that you will give me a heart to discern and accept your will for my life. I ask Father, that you would also empower me to live a healthy lifestyle in order to effectuate a conducive spiritual atmosphere for your healing anointing to flow into my body.

Father, I thank you for sending your Son, Jesus Christ who came to set me free from (name sickness). He personally carried my sins in His body on the cross, [willingly offering Himself on it, as on an altar of sacrifice], so that I might die to sin [becoming immune from the penalty and power of sin] and live for righteousness; for by His wounds, I believe, I have been healed.[204] I receive with thanksgiving the free gift of healing, and deliverance. I acknowledge and believe that Jesus Christ paid the price for my healing over two thousand years ago way before these symptoms appeared. I have this confidence that as I ask for healing and wholeness in my body according to your will, you will hear and answer me.[205] Because, you did not spare your Son – Jesus Christ, but delivered him up for my sake, you will with Him also give me all things.[206] I therefore, ask for healing, wholeness, and restoration in my body in the name of Jesus Christ of Nazareth, that my joy may be full.[207]

I refuse to accept the FACTS that I see and feel. I choose to receive the TRUTH of my healing. This sickness of (name of sickness) is a thief that has come to steal, kill, and destroy. And I declare that Christ has given me abundant life.[208] It is the Spirit who gives life; the flesh profits nothing. The words of God being spoken over me

---

[203] Luke 11:12-13.
[204] 1 Peter 2:24 (AMP).
[205] 1 John 5:14-1.
[206] Romans 8:32.
[207] John 16:23-24.
[208] John 10:10.

are spirit and life.[209] I declare that the life of God is flowing through my body right now, and bringing healing to all the intricate parts of my being. Every cell, organ, and tissue in my body are aligning to the word of life; and I command them to function perfectly according to the word of God in the name of Jesus. Jesus Christ bore my griefs and carried my sorrows. He was wounded for my transgressions (sins), he was bruised for my iniquities (moral evils), and the chastisement (correction or discipline) that procured my peace with God was placed upon him, and with his stripes (wounds), I declare – I am healed, cured, and made whole,[210] in the name of Jesus Christ of Nazareth. He sent His word and healed me, and delivered me from my destructions.[211]

I rebuke the spirit of infirmity attached to this sickness/disease of (name sickness); and I rebuke the spirit of death hovering over my life in the name of Jesus Christ. I shall not die but live and declare the works of the Lord here on earth, in the name of Jesus Christ.[212] By the authority of the Almighty God, I command this sickness of (name sickness) in my body to hear the voice of God and bow its knees in the name of Jesus Christ. I bind the root spirit of deaf and dumb. I command this sickness to die from its roots. I uproot it, I cut it, I break its hold from my life and along with the evil spirits attached to it, I send them to dry places in the name of Jesus Christ of Nazareth. I cover myself with the blood of Jesus Christ. I thank you Lord for my healing, restoration, and wholeness. I thank you for hearing me in the name of Jesus Christ of Nazareth - your Son, amen! I plead the blood of Jesus Christ over me and my loved ones for our wholeness in Jesus name.

---

209 John 6:63.
210 Isaiah 53:4-6.
211 Psalm 107:20 (NKJV).
212 Psalm 118:17.

Declaration of Healing

I plead the blood of Jesus Christ over all the intricate parts of my entire body. I declare over my body that I am healed because; every good and perfect gift comes from above, and from the Father of lights, with whom there is no variableness, neither shadow of turning.[213] I declare my freedom from fear and doubt for God is with me. I refuse to be dismayed. God is strengthening me and helping me. He is upholding me with the right hand of His righteousness.[214] I declare that God did not give me the spirit of fear, but He has given me His Spirit of power, of love, and sound mind.[215] I declare that my body is as healthy as my soul is prosperous[216] in the name of Jesus Christ.

My Father, I thank you for restoring health unto my body, and healing me of all my wounds in Jesus name.[217] I thank you for healing me and curing me from this sickness of (name of sickness). I thank you for revealing unto me the abundance of your peace and truth.[218] I thank you Lord, that as I walk in your statutes, and keep your commandments, and do them, you are making me fruitful, multiplying, and establishing your covenant with me for good.[219] Because I am your child and walk in obedience to your word, I declare over my life in agreement to your word that: my light is breaking forth as the morning, my health is springing forth speedily, and my righteousness is going before me; and the glory of the Lord shall continuously be my reward.[220]

---

213 James 1:17.
214 Isaiah 41:10.
215 2 Timothy 1:17.
216 3 John 2.
217 Jeremiah 30:17.
218 Jeremiah 33:6.
219 Leviticus 26:3-9.
220 Isaiah 58:8.

My Father, It pleases you that I prosper and live in good health even as my soul prospers.[221] It gives you great pleasure that *I am healthy and enjoy good health; to be safe and sound in spirit, soul, and body; to be well, cured, freed, and healed; to have a way opened for me; to go well with me and everything that concerns me always, continuously everywhere, all over, publicly, regularly, completely, day by day, in great depth, in great endurance, in great humility, and in great patience; in a profound, secure, and sufficient manner forever, even as my soul prospers,*[xi] in Jesus name, amen! It pleases you to bless me in all areas of my life therefore; I align myself with your promise of wellness in spirit, soul, and body. Not for me alone, but for the sake of your kingdom. Let the Lord be magnified because, my prosperity brings him pleasure.[222] Thank you my Father, for you have given me your Holy Spirit and have not left me comfortless or as an orphan.[223] Mighty One, you are a God that loves his children and cares for their every need.

My God, though, hard times may well be the plight of the righteous— *they may often seem overwhelmed*— but the Eternal rescues the righteous from what oppresses them.[224] My hope is in you my God. I will continue to praise you, for you are the health of my countenance. I will not be overwrought; I will not be disturbed. I will just hope in my God. Despite all my emotions, I will believe and praise the One who saves me – my God.[225] I declare over my life that, my days shall be multiplied, and the years of my life shall be increased in Jesus name.[226] I shall not die before my time.[227] Rather, by reason of God's strength

---

221 3 John 2.
222 Psalm 35:27.
223 John 14:25-28.
224 Psalm 34:19 (VOICE).
225 Psalm 42:11 (VOICE).
226 Proverbs 9:11.
227 Ecclesiastes 7:17.

upon my life, I shall live a long and fruitful life,[228] and I shall come to my grave in a full age, like as a shock of corn comes in his season in the name of Jesus Christ.[229]

God's blessings follow and await me at every turn because: my focus is on Him and His righteousness; because I do not follow the advice of those whose delight is in wicked schemes; I avoid sin's highway; and refuse to beckon on the call of judgment and sarcasm; because the Eternal's Word is my happiness and my focus is on His Word from dusk to dawn. I am like a tree planted by flowing, cool streams of water that never run dry. My fruit ripens in its time; my leaves never fade or curl in the summer sun. I am still yielding righteous fruit to the glory of God. No matter what I do, I am prospering in all areas of my life in the name of Jesus Christ.[230]

I declare over my life – no evil will befall me; no harm will come near my dwelling. The Lord has given his angels charge over me to keep me in all my ways. They shall bear me up in their hands, lest I dash my foot against a stone. I am treading upon the lion and adder; and I trample on the young lion and dragon under my feet. Because the Lord has set his love upon me, he has delivered me. He has placed me on high because I know his name. When I call upon him, he will answer me. He is with me in trouble, he will deliver me at all times and honor me. And with long life will he satisfy me and show me his salvation in Jesus name, amen![231] Because I wait upon the Lord my God, he is renewing my strength. I am mounting up on wings as eagles; I am running and not weary, I am walking and not fainting,[232] because the joy of the Lord

---

228 Psalm 90:10.
229 Job 5:26.
230 Psalm 1.
231 Psalm 91:10-16.
232 Isaiah 40:31.

will continue to be my strength.[233] I declare that, the Lord will continue to be my salvation, my glory, and the rock of my strength, and my refuge,[234] for all eternity, amen!

Now, begin to follow this prayer of faith and declaration with action, and do the things you have not been able to do before.

---

233 Nehemiah 8:10.
234 Psalm 62:7.

Write down your Testimony and Answers to Prayers

CHAPTER 3

Prayer for Completion of Project(s) and Breakthrough

Seemingly impossible situations call for drastic measures however; there are times when fasting has to be employed in order to achieve desired results.

~ *JOSEPHINE AKHAGBEME*

GOD DESIRES TO EMPOWER YOU in the completion of all that you lay your hands to do. What are the promises God has personally given you? Have they manifested yet? Can you see stagnation pattern in your life, finances, purpose and vision? Is there a revolving door of debt, living pay check to pay check, overdrawn bank account, not enough to pay bills, give tithes, or support the work of our Master Jesus Christ? Do you lack all the resources to complete the projects you have begun? Do these sounds familiar?

You may have given up hope because you have waited for so long for God to manifest his promises in your life. God may have given you, personal prophesies of what he will accomplish in your life and yet it has not manifested. You may have received visions and dreams about your future but it has not materialized yet. I want you to know that God has not forgotten, he will accomplish his Word to you and will not delay. God is saying to you today, "Write down this vision. Write it clearly on tablets, so that anyone who reads it may run. For the vision points ahead to a time I have appointed; it testifies regarding the end, and it will not lie. Even if there is a delay, wait for it. It is coming and will come without delay."[235]

POSITION YOURSELF FOR BREAKTHROUGH

In order to experience breakthrough, you have to position yourself. The way you position yourself in the word of God determines what happens to you in what you are experiencing. The word of God is spirit and life.[236] Therefore, everything about your situation rest on the word of God. It is all about the measure of the word of God in your life. How much word of God do you possess in your heart? Are you unmovable, unshakable, or unperturbed by situation around you? As a man thinks in his heart, so is he.[237] Your trust in God will cause you to be cognizant of the fact that in the midst of chaos, "you will not be afraid of evil tidings: your heart is fixed, trusting in the LORD."[238] When you hide God's word in your heart, it will prevent you from sinning against Him[239] through unbelief, faithlessness, doubt, or fear.

You cannot experience breakthrough without the empowerment of the Holy Spirit. You need wisdom, understanding, and insight in order to experience breakthrough. Wisdom, understanding, counsel, might, and knowledge are embodied in the person of the Holy Spirit[240]

---

235 Habakkuk 2:2-3 (VOICE).
236 John 6:63.
237 Proverbs 23:7.
238 Psalm 112:7.
239 Psalm 119:11.
240 Isaiah 11:2.

and without Him, you cannot experience lasting breakthrough. The Holy Spirit who is the teacher and revealer of secrets, will teach you all things and bring all things to your remembrance.[241] Because of the indwelling of the Holy Spirit in our lives, God's "divine power has bestowed on us [absolutely] everything necessary for [a dynamic spiritual] life and godliness, through true *and* personal knowledge of Him who called us by His own glory and excellence.[242]

It is impossible to be a Holy Ghost - filled Christian and fail. Failure is not an option in God's kingdom. When you position yourself spiritually by reading God's word; memorizing scriptures; praying; trusting God that he has you where you are; believing that he has heard your prayers and is in control; and when you rid your mind of all doubts, fear, worries, and anxiety, you cannot fail. Is there anything too difficult for God? "Who stirred up one from the east, calling him in righteousness to his service? He hands nations over to him and subdues kings before him. He turns them to dust with his sword, to windblown chaff with his bow. He pursues them and moves on unscathed, by a path his feet have not traveled before."[243] If you are experiencing failure in your life right now, examine yourself and begin to call upon the Lord and he will show you great and mighty things you do not know or understand.[244] He will direct you by His Spirit on what to do next.

God is not the author of failure because, failure does not exist in the kingdom of heaven. It is the devil who wants you to fail and not fulfill your destiny and purpose in life. Beloved, if you are failing, it is not God, it is you. You actually positioned yourself knowingly or unknowingly to fail because, it starts from your heart. You have to reposition yourself to overcome and it starts in your heart – what you believe.

---

241 John 14:25-27.
242 2 Peter 1:3 (AMP).
243 Isaiah 41:1-3 (NIV).
244 Jeremiah 33:3.

You have to determine to win and prosper spiritually and physically because, God's "divine power has given us everything we need for a godly life through our knowledge of him who called us by his own glory and goodness."[245] Your ability to grasp this truth will galvanize you above your peers to a higher level of breakthrough.

The Holy Spirit is waiting to give you insight that only Him possess. The problem is that you have not asked him. You can ask him right now and he will guide you. What insight do you need in your situation? Through the word of God, you get understanding. The word of God is a lamp unto our feet, and a light unto our path.[246] Don't let it be said of you "fools and their folly are promoted to positions of authority, while the rich and talented are assigned menial tasks. I have seen slaves riding on horseback like royalty and princes walking on the ground like slaves.[247] You have the ability to exercise dominion in all areas of your life through the Holy Spirit in you. You have to realize that, God's breakthrough in your life is for God's kingdom and as such, he desires to exponentially bless you for his Glory as well as for your good.

RIGHT MOTIVE IN PRAYER

Some Christians have their priority mixed up by pursuing after fleeting riches of the world. The bible encourages us to seek first the kingdom of God, and his righteousness; and all the things the world is after will be added unto you.[248] Riches are not meant to be sought and pursued after, they are benefits of the kingdom, added by God only. The Lord already set a pattern of priority for us in what we should be pursuing after which is: the kingdom of God and his righteousness. This is be-

---

245 2 Peter 1:3 (NIV).
246 Psalm 119:104-106.
247 Ecclesiastes 10:6-7 (VOICE).
248 Matthew 6:32-34.

cause, those who search after God's kingdom and righteousness will possess the benefits of riches and honor. For the Lord says "I love those who love me; those who search hard for me will find me. Riches and honor are *the benefit of* following me; so are lasting wealth and justice. My reward is better than gold, even the purest gold; and my profit is greater than the highest quality silver."[249]

You do not seek after things meant to be additions (car, clothes, houses, money, food, promotion, or status) rather, you pray for souls, and kingdom work. God is aware that you have need of all that the world is seeking after. You please God by seeking first his kingdom and righteousness. The only things meant to be sought after are: God's kingdom and his righteousness. When you do that, he will hear you as his child.

> This is how it will be for people who accumulate huge assets for themselves but have no assets in relation to God. (then, to His disciples) This is why I keep telling you not to worry about anything in life—about what you'll eat, about how you'll clothe your body. Life is more than food, and the body is more than fancy clothes. Think about those crows flying over there: do they plant and harvest crops? Do they own silos or barns? *Look at them fly.* It looks like God is taking pretty good care of them, doesn't it? Remember that you are more precious to God than birds! Which one of you can add a single hour to your life or 18 inches to your height by worrying really hard? If worry can't change anything, why do you do it so much? Think about those beautiful wild lilies growing over there. They don't work up a sweat toiling for needs or wants—they don't worry about clothing. Yet the great King Solomon never had an outfit that was half as glorious as theirs! Look at the grass growing over there. One

---

249 Proverbs 8:17-19 (VOICE).

day it's thriving in the fields. The next day it's being used as fuel. *If God takes such good care of such transient things,* how much more you can depend on God to care for you, weak in faith as you are. Don't reduce your life to the pursuit of food and drink; don't let your mind be filled with anxiety. People of the world who don't know God pursue these things, *but you have a Father caring for you,* a Father who knows all your needs. *Since you don't need to worry—about security and safety, about food and clothing—*then pursue God's kingdom *first and foremost,* and these other things will come to you as well. My little flock, don't be afraid. *God is your Father, and* your Father's great joy is to give you His kingdom. That means you can sell your possessions and give generously to the poor. You can have a different kind of savings plan: one that never depreciates, one that never defaults, one that can't be plundered by crooks or destroyed by natural calamities. *Your treasure will be stored in the heavens,* and since your treasure is there, your heart will be lodged there as well.[250]

Praying the Heart of God

You seek God by going after what moves him – souls (humans). God breathed the breath of life into the nostrils of man (Adam), and he became a living soul.[251] Without the breath of God in us, we will not be alive "The spirit of God hath made me, and the breath of the Almighty hath given me life."[252] Just like God demands total and absolute worship of Him,[253] likewise, the devil is after worship which has been his

---

250 Luke 12:21-34 (VOICE).
251 Genesis 2:7.
252 Job 33:4 (KJV).
253 Exodus 34:14.

long-term goal,[254] and he seem to be getting a lot of it in our generation today from the media, music, fashion, lifestyle, etc. How long can people take God's grace for granted? "The Lord is not slack concerning his promise, as some men count slackness; but is longsuffering to us-ward, not willing that any should perish, but that all should come to repentance."[255]

God is glorified when you involve yourself in soul-winning, and you are kingdom-minded (and not stuff-minded), you will be blessed in so many ways. When you do what pleases God,[256] your prayers will be heard. Prayers that produce results include: praying for God to add souls into his kingdom; to use you to impact the world for his kingdom glory; for the earth to be filled with the knowledge of the glory of the LORD, as the waters cover the sea;[257] that people will know him, and the power of his resurrection, and the fellowship of his sufferings, being made conformable unto his death;[258] that God will anoint you to preach the gospel to the poor, to heal the brokenhearted, to preach deliverance to the captive, and recovering of sight to the blind, to set at liberty them that are bruised, and preach the acceptable year of the Lord.[259] Prayers like these touch the heart of God and produces results.

God's blessings in your life is all for his glory alone. If you are seeking God's blessings for your selfish ambition, he will not hear your prayers. it is all about the intent of your heart. You can successfully deceive people with your fake prayers, but God sees and knows the motive of your heart. A lot of Christians cannot get answers to their prayers because of the evil, wicked, and selfish motives of their hearts. "What

---

254 Isaiah 14:11-15.
255 2 Peter 3:9 (KJV).
256 John 8:29.
257 Habakkuk 2:14.
258 Philippians 3:10 (KJV).
259 Luke 4:18-19 (KJV).

causes fights and quarrels among you? Don't they come from your desires that battle within you? You desire but do not have, so you kill. You covet but you cannot get what you want, so you quarrel and fight. You do not have because you do not ask God. When you ask, you do not receive, because you ask with wrong motives, that you may spend what you get on your pleasures."[260]

In order to pray with results, you have to come to God with humility knowing that, it is because of the price Jesus paid on the cross of Calvary, which cleared the way for us to come before a Holy God. Jesus gave a parable of two men – one who came before God in prayer with a clean heart and the other with a prideful heart. "Two men went up to the temple to pray, one a Pharisee and the other a tax collector. The Pharisee stood by himself and prayed: 'God, I thank you that I am not like other people—robbers, evildoers, adulterers—or even like this tax collector. I fast twice a week and give a tenth of all I get.' "But the tax collector stood at a distance. He would not even look up to heaven, but beat his breast and said, 'God, have mercy on me, a sinner.' "I tell you that this man, rather than the other, went home justified before God. For all those who exalt themselves will be humbled, and those who humble themselves will be exalted.""[261] The motive of your heart has to be right before God in order to get results.

Riches are encapsulated in wisdom and understanding. You have to seek after wisdom and understanding in prayer, and meditating on the word of God with an intention to obey it. In the introduction, I talked about Isaac who was guided by God with wisdom and understanding, and when his riches were taken from him in the form of the wells he dug, because he carried greatness inside of him, he was able to duplicate the resources of wells over and over again. No one can take

---

260 James 4:1-3 (NIV).
261 Luke 18:9-14 (NIV).

wisdom and understanding from you though, it is possible to take properties or any tangible things.

One of the ways to your breakthrough is to ask God for wisdom and understanding for insight and direction to sow on good grounds that will yield exponential returns and be able to duplicate this success regardless of the famine all around like the case of Isaac. Physical locality, situations, and circumstances does not determine God's breakthrough. There is no place for pride in the kingdom of God. If you are blessed, it is for God's kingdom and glory alone. You do not pray for greatness; you are already carrying greatness inside of you. Rather, you pray for wisdom and understanding to discover this greatness and apply it to your life.

Leverage the Storms of life to Soar Higher

One way to access your breakthrough is to leverage the storms in your life to your advantage in order to soar higher. You have to realize that God is in control and that all things work together for good to them that love God, to them who are the called according to his purpose.[262] The eagle is a good analogy in leveraging the storm for its advantage. The eagle goes in search of the storm. As soon as it sees the storm coming, it positions itself in the midst of the storm and allow the storm to carry it without exerting its strength or energy. The storm can be a negative destructive element as well as a positive element, depending on your mindset. As for the eagle, it uses the storm to its advantage. In the midst of the storm, the eagle positions itself calmly and deliberately, void of fear or anxiety. It does not manipulate the storm in any way. Rather, the storm carries the eagle higher where it soars to greater heights. The eagle in positioning itself, leverages the power of

---

262 Romans 8:28.

the storm and does not need to exert any energy to soar higher, the storm does all the work.

You can leverage the storms of life today. The situation you encounter, and the circumstances that are meant to destroy and discourage you, can all be used to your advantage. What are the storms you are faced with in your life right now? The Lord is saying to you: be still and know that I am God: I will be exalted among the heathen, I will be exalted in the earth.[263] Do not be afraid of evil tidings: let your heart be fixed, trusting in the Lord.[264] Put your trust in God: do not be afraid of what any man can do to you.[265] It is God that gives power to the faint; and to them that have no might, he increases their strength.[266] Weeping may last for the night, but shout of joy comes in the morning.[267] Therefore, rise up in the strength of your God. Rise up in the might of your King. Ask him to give you the strength and might you need to go through the storm in your life. It is He alone that "makes the storm a calm and gentle whisper, so that the waves of the sea are still and hushed."[268] Arise! Arise! Shout for joy because, victory is yours.

The storms you encounter in life develops your spiritual muscle; "Through Him we also have access by faith into this [remarkable state of] grace in which we [firmly and safely and securely] stand. Let us rejoice in our hope *and* the confident assurance of [experiencing and enjoying] the glory of [our great] God [the manifestation of His excellence and power]. And not only *this*, but [with joy] let us exult in our sufferings *and* rejoice in our hardships, knowing that hardship (distress, pressure, trouble) produces patient endurance; and endurance, proven

---

263 Psalm 46:10 (KJV).
264 Psalm 112:7.
265 Psalm 56:11.
266 Isaiah 40:29.
267 Psalm 30:5.
268 Psalm 107:29.

character (spiritual maturity); and proven character, hope *and* confident assurance [of eternal salvation]. Such hope [in God's promises] never disappoints us, because God's love has been abundantly poured out within our hearts through the Holy Spirit who was given to us."[269]

As Christians, we cannot avoid trials of this earthly realm. Many times, in my home, we encountered difficult situations, and if God had not stepped in, it would have been disastrous. In the past years, we were barely making ends meet. I and my husband had full time jobs however, we had all sorts of bills to pay and three children to feed and take care of. We did not qualify for any government benefits because, we barely crossed the threshold of families that need assistance. Lots of times, we barely had enough money for anything else other than bills, bills, and more bills. Sometimes, I would lay hands on my refrigerator and declare food to fill it up by faith. Back-to-school days were difficult for my kids especially with their long lists of items needed for school. I would take the list and go into my closet, and pray unto God to provide what was needed for the kids. This continued for a few years. In the midst of our storm, we had peace and hope, knowing that this too shall pass. It seemed like a long time but God who is forever faithful, provided in miraculous ways, sometimes, using people to bless us in so many ways. Our good Father knows what his children need to keep them moving forward in any storm of life. He is aware of all we need. Our testimonies are developed in the storms we encounter in life. Passing through the fire of the storms of life sure hurt. You can literally feel the heat of the fire and the pain; but God who is faithful, always find a way out. And he always works it all out for our good and for his glory, amen!

The moment we pledge allegiance to God Almighty as our Master, the hordes of demons are unleashed against us to frustrate our spiritual walk on this earth. Beloved, when you find yourself in trials, tribulations, persecution, sufferings, or pain of any kind, you should take a

---

[269] Romans 5:2-5 (AMP).

moment and ask the Holy Spirit to reveal to your heart what the purpose of your situation is, and pray for strength to go through; for surely God will work it all out for your good and to His glory. This is because, there are specific virtues that can only be acquired through our sufferings as a result of Christ. In speaking about the benefit of our many trials and hardships as Christians, James states:

> Don't run from tests and hardships, brothers and sisters. *As difficult as they are, you will ultimately* find joy in them; if you embrace them, your faith will blossom under pressure *and teach you true patience* as you endure. *And true patience brought on by* endurance will equip you to complete the long journey *and cross the finish line*—mature, complete, and wanting nothing. If you don't have all the wisdom needed *for this journey,* then all you have to do is ask God for it; and God will grant all that you need. He gives lavishly and never scolds you for asking. The key is that your request be anchored by your single-minded commitment *to God*. Those who depend only on their own judgment are like *those lost on* the seas, carried away by any wave or picked up by any wind. Those *adrift on their own wisdom* shouldn't assume the Lord will *rescue them or* bring them anything. *The splinter of* divided loyalty *shatters your compass and* leaves you dizzy and confused.[270]
>
>> Wisdom, as James understands it, is the ability to live life well and make good decisions. Wisdom doesn't come from old age or hard knocks. Wisdom begins with knowing and depending absolutely on God, who is never stingy when it comes to wisdom for those who seek it. He supplies all the wisdom we need when we ask. But when we try to go

---

270 James 1:2-8 (VOICE).

it alone—without God—trouble is around the corner (VOICE Commentary).

Ask the Holy Spirit to position you strategically to soar higher on wings as eagles above all the enemy's attacks meant to destroy you. As you soar on wings like eagles, the Lord will renew your strength. Just like the eagle, you will not exert your energy and strength. You will run and not grow weary, you will walk and not faint.[271] The Holy Spirit will begin to manifest in your life the dominion you have in Christ.

Valley

A valley is a plain – a deserted plain where nothing is happening. It is a place of inactivity; a place of stagnation; a dry place where nothing can be achieved; a hopeless place; a place where there is no nourishment, no vision or has clouded vision; a limited place where little can be achieved. It is a dead place where there is no forward acceleration. In this passage of the valley of dry bones in Ezekiel 37:1-14, there are major players involved – valley, very dry bones, Ezekiel, and God.

Valley may represent lots of things, and some may be present to withstand the purposes of God in one's life. As such, anyone in the valley is stagnant physically and spiritually. Valley may represent debt, poverty, an unclean place full of unclean spirits. It is therefore possible for both valley and very dry bones to be present in one's life. The enemy's plan is to keep your prayer life dormant and stagnant. He is fine with you just reciting one or two lines in prayer, and he is ok with you not utilizing the name of Jesus Christ when you pray. A lot of Christians cannot mention the name of Jesus Christ in their prayers, or they may end it with "in the name of god". I do not answer "amen" to such prayers because, I am not sure what god they are praying to. To differentiate

---
271 Isaiah 40:31.

my God from every other, is to pray in the name of His Son, Jesus Christ.[272] That is the only name every knee bow to. I have identified several steps to pierce through any obstacles that may exist in your life, which has the purpose to hinder your breakthrough, based on this chapter in Ezekiel.

STEPS TO BREAKTHROUGH — EZEKIEL 37:1-14

The important first step is to be able to identify the valley and dry bones in your life in order to pray strategically. Ezekiel was able to identify the valley and very dry bones (verses 1-2). In this passage, these represent the Israelites who were likened to these dry bones (verse 11). They as a people of God were nationally dead with no hope of restoration whatsoever. With the help of God, having identified the problem and hindrances, or obstacles to your breakthrough, what do you do from this point forward? God asked Ezekiel, can these bones live? Why would God ask the question he has answer to? This is because; he wants you to be aware of his power. To know that there is hope regardless of the hopeless situation that confronts you. God needs you and me to display and demonstrate his power through. He wants you to come into agreement with his plans for your life. You can limit his power in your life due to unbelief therefore, it is important to align with him in agreement with his word.

The second step is to realize our inability to do anything without God (verse 3). Realize that the battle belongs to God, and the victory is ours. Ezekiel realized he cannot accomplish anything without the power of the Almighty God. We cannot do anything without the help of God through His Holy Spirit. Our knowledge, experience, education, or smartness cannot be utilized in spiritual battle. The Lord is the

---

272 John 16:23.

one who fights our battle.[273] You may embark in battle without the help of God however, safety is not guaranteed because "the horse is prepared against the day of battle: but safety is of the Lord."[274] Without God on your side, you cannot win any battle; for if God, be for you no one can be against you.[275] God Almighty is greater than anyone or evil in the world.[276]

The third step is to utilize the word of prophesy or prophetic declaration (verse 4). Operate in a prophet ministry by prophesying over your valleys and identified needs. There is power in prophetically declaring God's Word over any situation or circumstances we may encounter in life. Ezekiel was speaking as a prophet. He was prophesying with a focus on restoration, encouragement, and the telling of future events concerning the nation of Israel; he prophesied on restoring covenant faithfulness of God in his promise to the house of Israel (verses 11-14). God has given his children the power and authority to prophesy and speak or declare as his prophets on earth. He has given us the power and authority to thread on serpents and scorpions.[277] And he has given you the power to decree a thing and it shall be established unto you, and God's light shall shine upon your ways.[278] Because the Spirit of the Lord lives inside you, you can as a prophet declare over your circumstances and situation to reverse for good in the name of Jesus Christ. You can speak to the dry bones in your life, your home, family, job, finances, etc. to turn around and resurrect and come to life in the name of Jesus Christ. God did not only tell Ezekiel to prophesy, but

---

273 2 Chronicles 20:15, 32:8.
274 Proverbs 21:31.
275 Romans 8:31.
276 1 John 4:4.
277 Luke 10:19.
278 Job 22:28.

He went further and gave him the words to declare. Death and life are in the power of the tongue and they that love it will eat of its fruit.[279]

The fourth step is to ask the Lord to release His Spirit to breathe life and victory over the valleys and mountains in your life. It is ok to speak life into any dead situation however, only God can cause things to turn around for good. Therefore, you have to realize who is in control here, and totally rely and trust in Him. There is no place for pride, but total dependence on God Almighty.

Spiritual Storage Graves

The valley in this passage was storage graves of dead men's bones. The devil has set up graves for God's people where he could compartmentalize their resources, finances, energy, strength, ideas, visions, zeal for God, health, relationships, etc. and control, or manipulate them with his wicked schemes; subjecting men to the fear of death. This evil compartment causes limitations, hindrance, and stagnation. But the good news is that Jesus, by experiencing physical death, was able to destroy the devil that had the power of death.[280] Praise God, Satan no longer has the authority to keep God's children bound in spiritual graves or compartments. And he no longer has the power to keep people in slavery due to fear of death, hallelujah! With this victory, death is no longer the ultimate end. Because of Jesus Christ, we can now experience a beautiful, blissful endless eternity with our creator, "who will wipe away all tears from our eyes; and there shall be no more death, neither sorrow, nor crying, neither shall there be any more pain;[281] this is what life is all about.

---

279 Proverbs 18:21.
280 Hebrews 2:14-15.
281 Revelation 21:3-4 (KJV).

Just like Jesus Christ died and rose again, we have this same hope, and when we pass through physical death, we will rise again and be with Jesus for all eternity, world without end, amen! This is the power that was stripped from Satan over God's children. We have the power and ability by the Spirit of God in us to reverse any situation. We must realize that the devil is operating from a defeated platform, and we as the children of God are operating from a higher victorious platform of authority.

To come out of the spiritual storage graves of the enemy in your life, begin to declare, speak, and prophesy over your current situation and circumstances that needs a change. Begin to command those graves in your life or your family, to open for the Lord has lifted you out of your graves. The Lord is saying to you - I have opened your graves, O my people, and brought you up, out of your graves. I have put my Spirit in you, and you shall live (verses 13-14).

The breath of the Lord contains the power of resurrection. This same power was present at the creation, when God breathe the breath of life on man and he became a living soul.[282] You must realize that you are victorious and that the devil is defeated already and has no power to keep you down because, God's "divine power has given us everything we need for life and godliness through our knowledge of him who called us by his own glory and goodness. Through these he has given us his very great and precious promises, so that through them we may participate in the divine nature and escape the corruption in the world caused by evil desires."[283] You cannot settle for less than what Jesus Christ paid for on the cross of Calvary. You must not short-change yourself and accept the lies of Satan. You must rise up in the might of the Lord your God. Change is possible and victory is assured.

---

282 Genesis 2:7.
283 2 Peter 1:3-4 (NIV).

We must recognize the ministry of the Holy Spirit in the miraculous workings of God. Ezekiel was operating in the prophetic when he began to prophesy and declare over those dead bones. God has also given you the power through His Holy Spirit to prophesy and declare over your situation or circumstances and command them to come alive. Command them to reverse for good in the name of Jesus Christ.

Prayer

Father, I ascend unto your throne room – your throne of holiness, righteousness and justice, by the blood of the Lamb and the name of Jesus Christ. I come to the court of heaven and bring before your presence these prayers. Before I call, you are answering, and while I am yet speaking, you have heard.[284] You are a God of justice - the foundation of your throne is righteousness and justice.[285] As I bring before you these prayers, answer me speedily according to thy will; for you said, I should call upon you in the day of trouble: and you will deliver me and I shall glorify you.[286] My hope and trust is in you. I bow my knees before Your Majesty. I can do nothing without you. My Father, every situation, circumstances, trials, tribulations, and all sicknesses and diseases that may exist in my life, are aligning themselves to the authority of the risen Christ – my Lord and Savior. They are bowing their knees before His Majesty – the King of all Kings, and Lord of all Lords; Elohim is His name.

Father, you are a God of completion, and this is my season of completion - the perfect number eight, the season of new beginnings. Because I do not follow the advice of the ungodly (those who delight in wicked schemes), or stand in the ways of sinners (by avoiding the

---

284 Isaiah 65:24.
285 Psalm 97:2.
286 Psalm 50:15.

highway of sin), or sit in the seat of the scornful (those who makes jest of God and all that concerns Him). But rather, I delight in the law of the Lord, and my focus is on His Eternal Word (by meditating on it day and night); careful to do according to that which is written in it - I am surely blessed. I am like a tree that is planted by the rivers of water that never run dry; my fruit ripens in its time and my leaves never fade or whither in the summer sun - I am yielding my fruit in my season. Even in my old age, I am yielding righteous and godly fruit to the glory of God.

Father, I begin to align myself in agreement with your Word – thy Word is truth.[287] Let every man be a liar, but God be true.[288] I align myself with what you came to manifest on my behalf – I am free, I am delivered, I am prosperous, I am healed, I am an overcomer, I am victorious, I have the Shalom - Peace of God, and I am saved. I silent every contrary voice of opposition against my life, and every voice of condemnation in the name of Jesus Christ of Nazareth. My Father, I position myself in you by trusting in your word of truth. I pray that every sphere of my life will begin to experience breakthrough in the name of Jesus Christ. My Lord, let your word begin to launch me into my breakthrough as you leverage all situation and circumstances around me for my good and your glory. I pray that the enemy will not have the last say in my life. That he will not prosper over me for "the Lord will cause my enemies that rise up against me to be defeated before me; they will come against me one way, but flee before me seven different ways in confusion.[289]

My Lord, I pray that your wisdom and understanding through your Holy Spirit will guide my path; and it will not be said of me "I have seen slaves on horseback, while princes go on foot like slaves.[290] I pray that

---

287 John 17:17.
288 Romans 3:4a.
289 Deuteronomy 28:6-8.
290 Ecclesiastes 10:7.

you my Father, will continuously guide me by your Spirit of truth.[291] My Father, as I hide your word in my heart, I will not sin against you.[292] I ask you Father, that you will show me great and mighty things I do not know as I call upon your Holy name.[293] My Father, give me the treasures of darkness, and hidden riches of secret places for the work of your kingdom.[294] Blessed be the Lord, who daily loads me with benefits, even the God of my salvation.[295] Thank you my Father, for you have blessed me with all spiritual blessings in heavenly places in Christ.[296] My God, let your word begin to illuminate my path to breakthrough and let every darkness begin to diminish before me because, "I gain understanding from your precepts; therefore, I hate every wrong path. Your word is a lamp for my feet, a light on my path. I have taken an oath and confirmed it, that I will follow your righteous laws."[297]

I begin to declare the truth of your Word over my life, over my season, and over all that concerns me — hear the Word of the Lord God Jehovah. ALL that I am involved in, with my hands and heart in this season of mine, is prospering in the name of Jesus Christ of Nazareth.[298] I am planted in the Holy Spirit; I am planted in the solid rock Jesus. I am planted in God Almighty. Yeshua is His name, Elohim, Adonai, the glory and the lifter of my head. I refuse to be moved; I refuse to be shaken; I refuse to be swayed aside; I refuse to be bound; I refuse to stand still; I refuse to be stagnant; and I am coming out of the valley of dry bones right now in the name of Jesus Christ of Nazareth. I am moving forward and not backwards; I am alive; I am growing; I have life in

---

291 John 16:13.
292 Psalm 119:11.
293 Jeremiah 33:3.
294 Isaiah 45:3.
295 Psalm 68:19.
296 Ephesians 1:3.
297 Psalm 119:104-106 (NIV).
298 Psalm 1.

me; I am bringing forth my fruit unto righteousness; and the glory of the Lord is risen upon me.[299] In my season prosperity has come, in my season wealth has come; and in my season grace has come – to God be all the glory forever and ever, Amen! I apply the blood of Jesus Christ over me and my loved ones for our wholeness in Jesus name.

Dry Bones Arise

The enemy is attempting to penetrate our finances and resources. He is attempting to limit our ability, and compartmentalize our freedom to operate. His purpose is to steal, kill, and destroy. He is attempting to hinder us from being effective in God's kingdom in so many ways, so we cannot be effective in our sphere of jurisdiction. He is attempting to steal from us so he can control and manipulate us. But I declare that, he is a liar and a loser. He lost the battle over our lives way back on Calvary. But today is the day of our freedom and liberty. Today is our day of restoration. We have come to take back all that belong to us that the enemy have stolen. We have come to retrieve from the storage of the valley of dry bones what the enemy stole from us and take back – our families, our children, our marriages, our ministries, our careers, our wealth, our IQ, our health, our businesses, our homes, our neighborhoods, our sanity of minds, our peace, and all that concerns us, that Christ procured on our behalf on the cross of Calvary. Your desire determines your limit and how far you can go. If you desire to see a change in your situation, pray this prayer with me now.

Prayer

Every spiritual storage built by the enemy holding my health, resources and breakthrough, I command you to open right now in the name of

---
299 Isaiah 60:1.

Jesus Christ. I command every spiritual chain and lock to be broken and shatter in the name of Jesus Christ. Jesus Christ came to set the captives free and Satan has no right to hold me bound any longer. I have come to declare my freedom and liberty. I am free in the name of Jesus Christ. I have come to declare, from this day forward, I will live my full potential that Christ manifested on the cross of Calvary on my behalf. If God be for me, who can be against me?[300] The angel of the LORD encamps around me and delivers me because of the fear I have for God.[301]

My Father, as for me and my lineage, because of the blood of your covenant with me in Jesus Christ, you are freeing my prisoners from the waterless pit. You are setting free all that belong to me which the enemy has bound, tied up, confined, obligated, imprisoned, harnessed, hitched up, held captive, and tethered. By your power, the prisoners of hope are returning to their fortress. Father, I thank you because, you are restoring to me all that the enemy have stolen twice as much in the name of Jesus Christ.[302]

In my old age, I am still yielding forth righteous fruit – winning souls for Jesus Christ and bringing glory to His Holy name. With long life, will he satisfy me;[303] for length of days, and long life, and peace, shall the Lord add to me. Length of days is in His right hand.[304] I have come to impact my generation with the truth of the good news of the gospel of Jesus Christ – the gospel of salvation, the gospel of hope, the gospel of renewal, the gospel of restoration, the gospel of peace, the gospel of revival, the gospel of reconciliation, the gospel of deliverance, the gospel of healing, the gospel of freedom, and the gospel of liberty.

---

300 Romans 8:31.
301 Psalm 34:7.
302 Zechariah 9:11-12.
303 Psalm 91:16.
304 Proverbs 3:2, 16.

The joy of the Lord will continue to be my strength as I preach the good news of his kingdom.[305] For by Him, my days shall be multiplied, and the years of my life shall be increased.[306] Even to my old age, He will remain my faithful God – EL Emunah:[307] and will carry me through and deliver me. You Oh Lord give power to the faint; and to them that have no might, you increase strength. Even the youths shall faint and be weary, and the young men shall utterly fall. But because I wait upon the Lord, you are renewing my strength. I am mounting up with wings as eagles. I am running and not weary. I am walking and not fainting,[308] because you are my God, Jehovah Ma'ozi – The Lord my strength.[309]

My God arise let your enemies scatter before you. Arise oh God; let all those that are incensed against you fall for your sake. Arise Oh God, in your Might and power on my behalf. This is my season and I have come to my season of greatness. God has given me his Divine Capacity to house his Greatness in my life. Every dry and dead bone in my season that represents stagnation and limitation, and every withered leaf in my season that represents unfruitfulness, hear the Word of the Lord. Thus, says the Lord God who created you with life, come from the four winds, O breath of God, and breathe life into any spiritual stagnation and limitation in my life. I prophesy to the living winds, O breath of God – Holy Spirit, cause your breath of life to enter every area of my life. Lord, infuse your breath of life in all that concerns me in the name of Jesus Christ. I command every foul spirit of the valley to release all that Satan have stolen and compartmentalized, and all the resources God has given unto me to further the advancement of His

---

305 Nehemiah 8:10.
306 Proverbs 9:11, 10:27.
307 Deuteronomy 7:9.
308 Isaiah 40:29-31.
309 Exodus 15:2.

kingdom. I command them right now to be released unto me in the name of Jesus Christ of Nazareth. I apply the blood of Jesus Christ over me and my loved ones for our wholeness in Jesus name.

I Prophesy

Surely the Lord God has caused breath to enter into me now. I prophesy life over me where there is death in the name of Jesus Christ. I prophesy increase and abundance in my life and home where there is lack in the name of Jesus Christ. I prophesy progressive acceleration forward over my life where there is stagnation in the name of Jesus Christ. I prophesy blessing over my life where there is curse in the name of Jesus Christ. I prophesy peace and unity in my life and home where there is confusion in the name of Jesus Christ. I prophesy enlargement where there is limitation in the name of Jesus Christ. I prophesy hope in my life where there is hopelessness in the name of Jesus Christ. I prophesy to every dead thing in my season, you are coming alive right now in the name of Jesus. I have no withered leaves in my season and in my life in the name of Jesus.

I declare greatness over my season; and I declare victory over my season. Lord, begin to open every grave in my season and bring me out in the name of Jesus Christ. Thank you Lord for your Spirit lives within me and gives me life. Father, I thank you, for you are stepping into my affairs and all that concerns me right now. Jehovah, you are stepping up your intervention in my life right now. You have made a way where there seems to be no way. You are raising ambush against all my enemies. I thank you EL Gibbor – The Mighty Warrior, The Victorious One, and man of war, your arm of flesh has won the battle on my behalf, and I give you all the praise.[310]

---

310 Ezekiel 37:1-14.

Season of Breakthrough

Prayer

I declare, this is my season of breakthrough and because I am seeking first the kingdom of God and his righteousness and refuse to worry and fear; all the things I have need of that the world is seeking after — food, clothing, shelter, love, joy, peace, affirmation, and acceptance, are being added unto me in the name of Jesus Christ.[311] As I seek the Lord, I will find him. And when I shall search for him with all my heart, he will visit me.[312] Lord, I am seeking and searching for you with all my heart. Lord, visit me and show me your vastness and glory. There is an open portal from heaven during this season of mine. The windows of heaven are open and Adonai is pouring out His blessings, favor, and wealth on all those who have their hands open. Father, my heart and hands are open and ready to receive and accept your blessings of abundance because; "those who listen to instruction will prosper; those who trust the LORD will be happy."[313] My Father, I listen to your instruction and I am prospering "Blessed be your Holy name for you have blessed me with all spiritual blessings in heavenly places in Christ."[314] Therefore, I open my mouth and with an expectant heart of faith, I declare these prayers over my season right now, in the name of Jesus Christ of Nazareth.

I declare that my storehouse is overflowing with abundance. For the Lord Jehovah satisfies my desires.[315] All that I shall eat is being added unto me because; I am seeking first the kingdom of God and His

---

311 Matthew 6:25-34.
312 Jeremiah 29:13.
313 Proverbs 16:20 (NLT).
314 Ephesians 1:3.
315 Psalm 145:16.

righteousness. There is plenty to sustain me and I am lacking nothing. Food is being given unto me, and my water is sure.[316] God which has fed me all my life, long unto this day, will continue to meet my needs.[317] He is feeding me according to the integrity of His Heart;[318] and will continue to provide my daily needs in Jesus name.[319] I will not fret; I will not worry about what to eat, drink, or wear, or for shelter. For as surely as the Lord feeds the birds of the air, and cloth the lilies of the valley, and as my faithful Father, He has taken care of all the details that concern me and will continuously provide.[320]

Adonai has opened the windows of heaven and his blessings are being poured out for me because, I am a tither and a giver.[321] My Father, continue to provide me good seed – resources to sow in diverse areas of your kingdom for your glory; for as I give generously and invest in acts of love and kindness, my gifts will yield high returns later. As I divide my gifts among many, not hoarding my goods but spreading them around, and being a blessing to others I may need much help in the days ahead.[322] Lord, give me the wisdom to invest on good grounds that will yield abundant returns. Protect my investments with your power, and give me the heart not to trust in worldly riches but rather, put my trust in you. I rejoice, because my season of breakthrough is here. Your Majesty, Arise! Arise! In your Pomp and Glory; Arise! Arise! My King, be gloriously lifted up in my season. Be exalted in my season. Arise! Arise! Your Majesty, Arise with your vast abundance over my season in the name of Jesus Christ of Nazareth.

---

316 Isaiah 33:16.
317 Genesis 48:15.
318 Psalm 78:72.
319 Matthew 6:11.
320 Luke 12:22-31.
321 Malachi 3:10.
322 Ecclesiastes 11:1-2.

I declare over my season - hear the Word of the Lord. I speak life over you in Jesus name. I declare over my season - Grace! Grace! Peace! Peace! I declare completion over you. I declare increase and enlargement over you; for the Lord, has enlarged my steps under me so that my feet did not slip.[323] I declare excellence over you my season. The hand of the Lord is with me and He is continuously keeping me from evil.[324] The Lord is perfecting all that concerns my family, my destiny, my purpose, and all the projects I have begun. I declare favor of God over my season. I declare all that I need for life and godliness has been provided for already by His divine power.[325] The Sovereign LORD is my strength, he makes my feet like the feet of a deer, he enables and empower me to walk on heights in progressive strides.[326]

I begin to call into manifestation - finances and resources from the north, south, west and east to complete this (project name) in Jesus name. My God has given me the power to get wealth because; He has established His covenant with me in His Son Jesus Christ – my Lord and Savior.[327] Lord, you are revealing to me hidden treasures and wealth stored in secret places,[328] by your Holy Spirit who is the revealer of secrets.[329] I declare over my financial storehouse - bring forth resources, and spring forth speedily. I declare (project name) complete in the name of Jesus Christ of Nazareth.

I begin to declare greatness over my season. God has given me beauty for ashes, and the oil of gladness for mourning, the garment of praise for the spirit of heaviness. I am called a tree of righteousness, and

---

323 2 Samuel 22:37.
324 1 Chronicles 4:10.
325 2 Peter 1:3.
326 Habakkuk 3:19.
327 Deuteronomy 8:18.
328 Isaiah 45:3 (VOICE).
329 Daniel 2:47.

the planting of the Lord, that he might be glorified.[330] The Lord beautifies my destiny with salvation, and has taken away from me all ugliness of sorrow and pain in the name of Jesus Christ.

I have come into my season of increase, of moving forward and not backwards. I have come into my season of fatness; my season of peace and joy; my season of great anointing; my season of wealth; my season of salvation; my season of goodness and mercy; my season of plenty; my season of health; my season of strength and vigor; my season of prosperity and blessings; my season of yielding godly and righteous fruit; and my season of abundance of favor, boldness, fearlessness, and faith in the name of Jesus Christ. God is elevating me to a new and higher level of greatness in Him. The impossible is taking place right now in my life, and His time to favor me has come in the name of Jesus Christ of Nazareth.

Every hindrance to the completion of this (project name), I nullify and render you ineffective. Every mountain of hindrance, I command you to be removed out of my way and be annihilated in the name of Jesus Christ of Nazareth. I declare - no weapon that can hurt me has ever been forged, and nothing of the enemy will ever prosper over my life or against my finances; and no voice raised to condemn me will successfully prosecute me, be it in the witches' coven, in hell, land or sea; they will never succeed. These are not allowed to hurt me. They are condemned already, proven false, proven wrong, and I refute them in the name of Jesus Christ of Nazareth. This is my inheritance as a servant of the Lord, for the Lord shall continuously and ceaselessly vindicate me.[331]

I have the victory because I am a blood-bought saint of The Most High God who dwells on High. Silver and gold and all resources belong

---

330 Isaiah 61:3.
331 Isaiah 54:17

to God; He is Jehovah Jireh - my great provider.[332] The earth is His and I am his child therefore; I declare - it is well with me![333] It is well with my family; it is well with my home and properties; it is well with my marriage; it is well with my relationships; it is well with my children; it is well with my finances, and it is well with all that concerns me, in the name of Jesus Christ of Nazareth, amen! I apply the blood of Jesus Christ over me and my loved ones for our wholeness in Jesus name.

ADVANCING GOD'S KINGDOM AND RIGHTEOUSNESS THROUGH TITHES AND OFFERING

From the beginning, tithing was not meant to be a command. You are expected to give out of a willing heart and cheerful spirit. Abraham gave to Melchizedek tithes of his bounties and was blessed.[334] Later, it was changed into a commandment.[335] All the tithes belongs to the Lord and it is Holy unto Him.[336] Holy things belong to a Holy God and cannot be kept for ourselves. If we keep Holy things, it becomes a curse. He owns the tithes and we are only honoring Him with what belongs to Him, so we can connect to the blessings that come with tithing. God's blessings of abundance and increase are attached to tithes and offerings.[337] If you are not a tither, you are giving the devil a legal ground to mess up your finances and open the doors for other curses. We ought to give God what belongs to God – His tithes.

God desires to bless His children in all areas of their lives. In order to do that, we ought to obey His Word and commandment.

---

332 Genesis 22:14.
333 Haggai 2:8.
334 Genesis 14:18-24.
335 Deuteronomy 26:10-19.
336 Leviticus 27:30.
337 Malachi 3:8-12.

We have to repent from not offering God His Holy tithes and ask Him to forgive us. He is still redeeming and restoring today. We also have to ask Him to provide good seed to sow. Seed is meant to be planted on good ground that will produce bountiful harvest. You do not eat seeds meant to produce a harvest. Seed is given to a sower who will sow these seeds and allow them to grow and produce a harvest. When you tithe, God stops the devil from hindering your harvest. He protects the seed in order to germinate and produce abundance of harvest unto you.

Tithing also causes transference of wealth. God causes the wealth of the wicked to be transferred to you because; you have been proven as a faithful steward of God's Holy tithes.[338] When you tithe, wealth will be supernaturally transferred to you for the sake of the kingdom, and in the advancement of the good news of the gospel to the entire world. In addition, God will rebuke the devourer from coming to steal all that belong to you. God will supernaturally send healing to your body when needed and according to His Will; you will supernaturally accomplish your projects to completion; you will be blessed spiritually and physically.

God never created anything twice. He also created the seed to continuously reproduce and multiply because; the seed has multiplication encapsulated in itself. The Lord is the one that provides seed for the sower and bread for eating. He alone will provide and multiply your resources for sowing and increase the fruits of your righteousness which manifests itself in active goodness, kindness, and charity. Thus, you will be enriched in all things and in every way, so that you can be generous, and your generosity as it is administered will bring forth thanksgiving unto God.[339] This is why tithes are Holy unto God; it is used to honor God, it brings glory unto Him, it is used as a connection with

---

338 Proverbs 13:22.
339 2 Corinthians 9:10-11 (AMP).

the blessings of God, and for the work of the ministry. Additionally, God uses your tithe as a point of contact to manifest his goodness in your life.

PRAYER

Father, I thank you for your promise of wealth in Deuteronomy 8:18. You have given me the power to create wealth. Father, as I pay my tithes and offerings, you are pouring out your abundance in great measure unto me – pressed down, shaken together, and running over.[340] I thank you because, men will give unto me, and you will cause them to do good to me. I thank you for all the creative ideas that you have given me. I pray for divine wisdom to know how to activate these creative ideas so that I can be about my Father's business.

Father, as I intentionally seek first your kingdom and your righteousness, all other things I have need of are being added unto me in abundance right now, for the work of the ministry in the name of Jesus Christ of Nazareth.[341] Father, I thank you as I give into your kingdom through tithes and offerings, you are unlocking closed doors, and connecting me to the treasures of heaven. I thank you for the keys of the kingdom of heaven is mine. I therefore utilize these keys in binding and loosing through declarations to align with your will in heaven. I acknowledge that, The LORD our God is one LORD. Father, teach me how to love you with all my heart, and with all my soul, and with all my might, amen![342] I apply the blood of Jesus Christ over me and my loved ones for our wholeness in Jesus name.

---

340 Luke 6:38.
341 Matthew 6:33.
342 Deuteronomy 6:4-5.

Blessed in Giving

Prayer

Lord I thank you for the opportunity to be blessed in giving and partnering with you. I thank you for providing the right seed to sow into your kingdom in order to be blessed.[343] As I honor you Lord with my possessions, finances, and house, my bank account will not be overdrawn. I will always have enough to pay my mortgage, and pay it off completely. In your abundant provision, I will always have enough to give to the advancement of the gospel of Jesus Christ on this earth. As I honor you Lord with all I have, new ideas for business is being released to me. Open doors and divine connection ministry-wise, business-wise, financial-wise, are released unto me.[344]

Father, I understand that you have set before me life and death, blessing and cursing. I choose life that I and my lineage and blood line may live.[345] All the blessings that accompany your command to tithe and give offerings are following me. You are holding back the hand of the devourer, protecting my assets and everything that belongs to me. You have cancelled all the sixteen poverty curses, and fifty-four sickness curses from my life.[346] Your divine protection is over my life and property in Jesus name, amen!

My Father, I thank you for every door you have ordained to be opened, is beginning to open unto me right now in the name of Jesus Christ. I declare to every doors and gates of blessings "Lift up your heads, you gates; be lifted up, you ancient doors that the King of glory may come in. Who is this King of glory? He is the Lord Strong and

---

343 Malachi 3:6-10, Leviticus 27:30-32.
344 Proverbs 3:9-10.
345 Deuteronomy 30:19.
346 Deuteronomy 28.

Mighty, the Lord Mighty in battle. Lift up your heads, you gates; lift them up, you ancient doors that the King of glory may come in. Who is He, this King of glory? The Lord Almighty—He is the King of glory.[347] I am in the right place and in the right time in my season and I am yielding righteous fruit to the glory and praise of God Almighty, in the name of Jesus Christ of Nazareth.

Father, I thank you for the ability to give and sow into your kingdom. I thank you that as I give, you are opening your floodgates of heaven and pouring out so much blessing in abundance unto me. I thank you for rebuking and preventing the devourer for my sake. I thank you for preventing the destructive pests of any kind to destroy all that I am blessed with.[348] I thank you for divine protection upon all areas of my life. I thank you for taking away the curses of poverty from my life. I thank you Father, for connecting me to the blessings of tithes and offering. I thank you for providing the right seed to sow into your kingdom.

Lord I thank you for as I continue to support the work of your kingdom in giving, I am blessed; and your ability not to judge or condemn but to forgive is manifesting in my life. Your ability to give generously in my life is increasing more and more in good measure, pressed down, shaken together and running over in Jesus name.[349] I thank you that you are watering the ground in order to produce a bountiful harvest for me. I thank you that your blessing in my life is not for me alone but for the advancement of your Kingdom on earth. I recognize that all things you have blessed me with are for your glory. I pray that you would give me eyes to see, ears to hear, and a heart to comprehend how you desire the blessing in my life to be channeled in Jesus name, amen!

I thank you Adonai for your gift of life. You came down to us as the creator – fully man and fully God. Father, I thank you for pouring all

---

347 Psalm 24:7-10 (NIV).
348 Malachi 3:10-12.
349 Luke 6:37-38.

my sin upon your Son – Jesus Christ though He was sinless. This is because; you have made me the righteousness of God in Christ.[350] Thank you for decorating my life with your righteousness, your holiness, your glory, your greatness, your love and peace. Thank you for making my life worth dying for. Thank you for the cross and the blood, and your name. Thank you Father for the great love you have for me. You love me so much that I am unable to adequately comprehend the depth of it all.

I give you praise Adonai because; the spirit of death has passed over me and my household as a result of the Blood of the Lamb. You will not allow the destroyer to come into my household to steal, to kill, and to destroy because, as a giver, I have abundant life in Jesus Christ my Master and Lord.[351] I honor you Adonai as I remember how you brought your people out of Egypt with your mighty outstretched hand. I give you thanks Adonai for bringing me out of spiritual Egypt along with its wealth and resources.[352] Thank you my Father for the completion of (project name) in good time and speedily in the name of your Son Jesus Christ of Nazareth. I apply the blood of Jesus Christ over me and my loved ones for our wholeness in Jesus name.

The Glory of God in my Life

Arise Oh God, arise with your arm of strength, arise with your arm of victory, and arise in your glory and majesty on my behalf. Majestic is your name in all the earth. There is no God like you. There is none to compare to you. You are the Alpha and Omega; you are the beginning and the end. You are glorious, you are exalted, you are magnificent, you are mighty, you are powerful, and you are honorable. There is no

---

350 2 Corinthians 5:21.
351 Exodus 12:23, John 10:10.
352 Exodus 12:51, 13:3.

Jehovah as our God. We serve a mighty God; we serve an awesome God. I declare victory over my life – I am victorious.

My Father and King, you have given me your glory through your Son Jesus Christ.[353] I pray that your glory may be revealed and made manifest in my life in the name of Jesus Christ of Nazareth. My Father, your glory upon my life separates me from everyone else. Rain down your glory upon me. Let your glory cover my home, my children, my marriage, and everything that concerns me. Fill me with your glory; cover me with your glory. I welcome your glory in my life: thank you Lord for your glory.

I declare that I am rising up and shinning with the brightness of the glory of the Lord. Darkness covers the earth; and people all are covered in darkness; but God will rise and shine on me. The Eternal's bright glory is shining on me as a light for all to see. Nations north and south, peoples ease and west will be drawn to my light. They will find purpose and direction by my light. In the radiance of my rising, I will enlighten the leaders of nations. Lord, I thank you for establishing for me, favorable circumstances of peace, and relief from trouble. Thank you for looking upon me with your favor. Thank you for giving me a positive, happy attitude in life. I have come to my new day; my dawning of light has come. Your glory Oh Lord is risen upon me, and I am rising and breaking forth,[354] in the name of Jesus Christ.

Elohim, you sit enthroned as King forever. You have given me unyielding and impenetrable strength. Jesus, you are in the Father, and I am in you, and you are in me.[355] You have blessed me with your peace - Shalom in the midst of chaos. You have clothed me with your favor and glory - *Your glory of honor, splendor, brilliance, glow, brightness, wealth, pomp, dignity, riches, vast abundance, respect, multiplication, increase, distinguished,*

---

353 John 17:22.
354 Isaiah 60:1-3 (VOICE).
355 John 14:20.

remarkable, and high esteem with God and man; and your glory of unity as you Elohim, are one.[356xi] You O Lord have clothed me with your glory and empowerment for kingdom mandate, in advancing the gospel of hope and peace to the world. I begin to redirect and channel all the Glory back to you, Your Majesty. I am rising and breaking forth in the name of Jesus Christ, amen!

Peace of Jerusalem

Prayer

I pray for the peace of Jerusalem, and I bless your people Israel. Lord, bless them with eyes to see, ears to hear, and an understanding heart to be aware that Yeshua is in their midst, and is made manifest to deliver them from their enemies. I pray that they will come to the realization of the salvation that Yeshua has established for us on the cross of Calvary. According to your word, all Israel shall be saved.[357] I pray O Lord that you would reveal unto them the abundance of peace, faith and truth "This people have you formed for yourself: they shall shew forth your praise."[358] They are a chosen generation, a royal priesthood, a holy nation, and God's special people; that they may proclaim the praises of Him who have called them out of darkness into His marvelous light.[359] Restore their city and heal the wounds of your people O Lord. Lavish them with peace and stability. Father, begin to send ambush against their enemies. Send confusion into the camp of their

---

356 John 17:22.
357 Romans 11:26.
358 Isaiah 4:21.
359 1 Peter 2:9.

enemies, and cause them to flee before your people. May all those that rise up against them fall for their sakes.

Lord, you are the hope of your people, and the strength of the children of Israel.[360] Bring both Judah and Israel completely back from captivity, and rebuild their land to what it was before.[361] Father, I thank you because you will gather your people Israel and bring them home.[362] Give unto them beauty for ashes, the oil of Joy for mourning, and the garment of praise for the spirit of heaviness.[363] Take away every stubborn heart of stone from your people and plant in them a new heart and a new spirit – a willing and tender heart of flesh, so that the gospel of Jesus Christ will penetrate their spirit and soul, and they will come to know the King of Kings, and the Lord of all Lords – Yeshua, Jesus Christ of Nazareth, amen![364] I plead and apply the blood of Jesus Christ over God's people in Jesus name.

Prayer for Missionaries

In praying for missionaries, if you know of any, use them as a point of contact by calling their names.

Father, I also pray for missionaries all over the world using (name of missionary), as a point of contact. My Father, send help to them. Raise ministry supporters for them. Father, may your ministering angels, minister strength unto them. May they never give up hope or be weary in well doing, for in the appointed time, they will reap goodness and

---

360 Joel 3:16.
361 Jeremiah 33:6-7 (VOICE).
362 Zephaniah 3:15-20.
363 Isaiah 61:3.
364 Ezekiel 36:26 (VOICE).

greatness.[365] I bless them with the blessings of the Lord. I bless them with the encouragement and peace that comes only from Yeshua. Lord, confirm their ministry with signs and wonders following them.

Father, send your healing balm of Gilead and heal their every wound, in the name of Jesus Christ.[366] Empower them greatly with your Spirit with signs and wonders following. Father, "spread out a table before them, because you care for all their needs provide for them in the midst of attacks from their enemies. Anoint their heads with soothing, fragrant oil, filling their cup again and again with your grace. Certainly, your faithful protection and loving provision will continually pursue them wherever they go, always and everywhere."[367]

Father, I pray for strength as they face death and imprisonment daily for the sake of the gospel of Jesus Christ. I pray that the hope of our calling will comfort them. Which hope we have as an anchor of our soul; this hope is both sure and steadfast, located in the highest of heavens. And Jesus Christ as our forerunner opened the way for us as our high priest, entered the Holies of Holies and that we might enter in with him.[368] I declare over them this hope, the peace of Yeshua and the strength of His might. I pray that they will not be weary in well doing; and because they wait upon the LORD and trust in His Holy name, their strength is being renewed in Jesus name. They are mounting up with wings as eagles; they are running and not weary; they are walking and not tired or fainting.[369]

Lord, send help to them as they continue to look unto Jesus, the author and finisher of our faith. He endured the cross and ignored the shame associated with that death, focusing on the joy that was before

---

365 Galatians 6:9.
366 Psalm 147:3.
367 Psalm 23:5-6 (VOICE).
368 Hebrews 6:19-20.
369 Isaiah 40:30-31.

Him; and now, he sits beside God on the throne, which is a place of honor.[370] I also pray that our God would count them worthy of this calling, and fulfil all the good pleasure of his goodness, and the work of faith and power: that the name of our Lord Jesus Christ may be glorified in them, and them in Him, according to the grace of our God and the Lord Jesus Christ.[371]

Father, I pray that they will find comfort in this hope, and will not count the cost but carry the message of the cross boldly and fearlessly to the world. For the preaching of the cross is to them that perish foolishness; but unto us which are saved, it is the power of God.[372] I pray Father, that your Holy Spirit will reveal the truth of your word to their hearts in the time of persecution. Those that are persecuted for righteousness sake are blessed; for the kingdom of heaven is theirs. When these are reviled, mocked, persecuted, and false accusations are brought against them for the sake of Jesus Christ, we rejoice, and we are exceedingly glad; for great is their reward in heaven.[373] Bless them and protect them for your name sake. Cover them with your glory and shield them from the enemy for the sake of the gospel of Jesus Christ. I thank you Lord for hearing me. To you Adonai, I give all the Glory both now and forevermore, Amen! I plead and apply the blood of Jesus Christ over missionaries all over the world in Jesus name.

---

370 Hebrews 12:1-3.
371 2 Thessalonians 1:11-12.
372 1 Corinthians 1:17-18.
373 Matthew 5:10-12.

Write down your Testimony and Answers to Prayers

CHAPTER 4

Restoration

Great people think "greatness" that carries them through difficult times.

~ JOSEPHINE AKHAGBEME

GOD IS STILL RESTORING AND redeeming today as he did in the days of old. God has blessed his people exponentially but they don't seem to be experiencing the fullness of His blessings. His children are wealthy yet, they cannot seem to grasp this wealth. His children are blessed with gifts and abilities that will yield financial and spiritual rewards and benefits yet, it seems to elude them. The Lord has made provision for healing in his revealed word yet, many believers are weighed down with all sorts of sicknesses and diseases, pain and suffering, disappointments and broken hearts. There are secrets that have been revealed to believers in the scriptures "the secret things belong to God, but those revealed truths are ours."[374] "Praise be to the God and Father of our Lord Jesus Christ, who has blessed us in the heavenly realms with every spiritual blessing in Christ. For he chose us in him before the creation of the world to be holy and blameless in his sight"[375]

---

374 Deuteronomy 29:29.
375 Ephesians 1:3-4 (NIV).

It is important to understand the great treasure God has established for his children – Christians. Grasping this truth will enable you in praying with results. The bible says "The house of the righteous contains great treasure, but the income of the wicked brings ruin."[376] The word for "treasure" in Hebrew is *Ḥōsen* which means: stored treasures, riches, and wealth. The same word in Aramaic is *Ḥᵉsēn* which means: power, might, force, and mighty. Related meaning of the word in Aramaic is: *Ḥᵃsēn* which means: to take possession of, and occupy. As a believer, God has given unto you the power and might, and the capacity and ability to be mighty. As a Christian, your home, household, family line, clan, tribe, or dynasty (linked to the Hebrew word *bayit*) has treasures, riches, and wealth.[xiii] Therefore, you have to take possession and occupy the place God has elevated you to be. You can only take possession of this wealth and riches through prayer with the understanding that, these are already provided for and you have to receive them in faith and belief. If you are not experiencing all that the Lord has provided, you will have to pray through; for surely, God desires for you to access his great treasure to impact the world and win souls for his glory.

God revealed to the children of Israel the conditions for restoration and blessings in Deuteronomy 28 and 30. In order to access these blessings, you will have to call to mind these words, remember, and obey the voice of God with all your heart and soul. I will briefly summarize the steps of restoration based on chapter 30.

Steps to Restoration – Deuteronomy 30

God revealed to the children of Israel conditions for restoration and blessings in this chapter. The blessings of the kingdom are only for the children of the kingdom.

---

376 Proverbs 15:6 (NIV).

The first step (verses 1-2) is to repent and remember to keep God's word in your *heart*. The Hebrew word for *heart* is *lēbāb*, and this denotes the seat of thought and emotion. It means to give careful thought, wholehearted devotion, to consider with purpose and convictions the word of God.[xiv] Let the word of God have a settlement in your heart that it becomes all you think about every moment. Meditate on it constantly by giving careful thought, wholehearted devotion, and considering it with a purpose and conviction. Let all your desires be to obey the word of God. Let it be in your heart that it becomes your heart beat because, "The time is fulfilled, and the kingdom of God is at hand: repent ye, and believe the gospel."[377]

The second step (verse 2) is to obey his voice through the revealed word of the Bible. Full obedience to God's word is required and not partial obedience. Obey the Lord with all thine heart, and with all thy soul. Not doubting his word, not entertaining fear, but have faith that his word is true and what he has promised, will be accomplished in your life. You have to have a mindset of possibility, a resolve that you will obey his word no matter what the outcome will be. One of the Hebrew word for *obey* is *sāma*. The meaning includes: to listen carefully to God's word, discerning what he is saying to you, comply and carry out the instructions contained in it, diligently obey, pay close attention to it with a purposeful intention to obedience, put under oath, and receive the message with a receptive mind.[xv] This will be executed in a deliberate intention of studying God's word with a purpose of knowing it and keeping it to heart in order to obey it.

The third step (verse 16) is to love the Lord thy God, walk in his ways, and keep his commandments, statutes and judgments. "And Jesus answered him, the first of all the commandments is, Hear, O Israel; The Lord our God is one Lord: And thou shalt love the Lord thy God with all thy heart, and with all thy soul, and with all thy mind, and with

---
377 Mark 1:15.

all thy strength: this is the first commandment. And the second is like, namely this, thou shalt love thy neighbor as thyself. There is no other commandment greater than these.[378]

The three key areas are: to love the Lord your God, walk in his ways, and keep his commandments.[379] In summary, all that is required of us is: to love the Lord thy God, listen and obey his voice, cleave unto him or hold fast to him. The Lord is your life, your breath, and your source of everything. For in him we live, and move, and exist.[380]

Prayer

Lord, I ascend unto your throne of Mercy and Grace, not by my righteousness – for they are filthy rags before you: but by the righteousness of your Son Jesus Christ. I come to your throne by the Cross, the Blood of Jesus, and the Name of Jesus Christ. Father, I come to you in humility knowing that my righteousness is filthy rags before your Holiness.[381] I thank you for your forgiveness. In your mercy temper justice with peace. Remove far from me all my sins, as far as the east is from the west, amen.[382] LORD, hear my prayer; listen to my cry for mercy; in your faithfulness and righteousness come to my relief. Answer me quickly, LORD; my spirit fails. Do not hide your face from me or I will be like those who go down to the pit. Let the morning bring me word of your unfailing love, for I have put my trust in you. Show me the way I should go, for to you I entrust my life.[383]

---

378 Mark 12:29-31 (KJV).
379 John 15:9-10.
380 Acts 17:28.
381 Isaiah 64:6.
382 Psalm 103:10-12.
383 Psalm 143:1, 7, 8 (NIV).

I choose to align myself with the truth of your Word: for all that you have spoken is already established – it is yea and amen. Let God be true, but every man a liar.[384] For the vision and message is for an appointed and set time. At the end, it will not lie, but shall speak and manifest. Though it tarries, I will patiently wait, because it will surely come.[385] I choose to believe your word of truth. I believe that all you have spoken will be made manifest in my life. Lord, empower me to keep your word in my heart in order to obey and do them. Help me to walk in your ways with honor and integrity of heart; to keep your commandments, statutes, and judgments. I confess that you O Lord our God, is One Lord. Teach me to love you with all my heart, soul, mind, and strength. Baptize me with your Spirit of love in order to love my neighbor as myself.

Father, I thank you because silver and gold belongs to you; all the earthly resources are yours.[386] "Yours, O Lord, are the greatness, the power, the glory, the victory, and the majesty; for all that is in the heavens and on the earth, is yours; yours is the kingdom, O Lord, and you are exalted as head above all. Riches and honor come from you, and you rule over all. In your hand are power and might; and it is in your hand to make great and to give strength to all. And now my God, I give thanks to you and praise your glorious name."[387] I thank you Father for depositing your power, capacity, and ability in me. I thank you for given me your great treasure, riches, and wealth.

I thank you because you have blessed me in order to advance your kingdom on this earth. I thank you Father, through me, all the resources you have blessed me with, will be used to preach the gospel of hope, reconciliation, peace, restoration, deliverance, healing, liberty

---

384 Romans 3:4.
385 Habakkuk 2:3.
386 Psalm 50:10, Haggai 2:8.
387 1 Chronicles 29:11-13 (NRSV).

and the revelation of the Messiah – The risen Christ on this earth. I am part of a chosen people, a royal priesthood, a holy nation, God's special possession, that I may declare the praises of him who has called me out of darkness into his wonderful light.[388] I thank you my Father that I overcome by the blood of the lamb and the word of my testimony.[389]

Father of glory, I ask you to give me understanding and discernment in knowing you personally. That my eyes will be focused and clear, so that I can see exactly what it is you are calling me to do; to grasp the immensity of this glorious way of life that you have for your children. Oh, the utter extravagance of your work in us who trust you – endless energy and boundless strength.[390] Elohim, you are great and mighty in power. Your understanding is infinitely limitless.[391] I apply the blood of Jesus Christ over me and my loved ones for our wholeness in Jesus name.

THE LAND OF THE LIVING

Generating money most times require a skill of some sort, and this skill require a careful deliberate process of learning and listening to the voice of God; But you shall remember [with profound respect] the Lord your God, for it is He who is giving you power to make wealth, that He may confirm His covenant which He swore (solemnly promised) to your fathers, as it is this day.[392] No knowledge is ever lost. Isaac learned the skill to generate money from his father's nomadic family trade. In addition, the Lord also had already trained him spiritually to hear and receive instructions from above. And when there was famine in the

---

388 1 Peter 2:9.
389 Revelation 12:11.
390 Ephesians 1:17-19 (MSG).
391 Psalm 147:5.
392 Deuteronomy 8:18 (AMP).

land, the Lord told him to immigrate into Egypt and dwell in the land of Gerar where he will be blessed, and be prosperous in the midst of famine. Having knowledge and the supernatural ability to discern and get wisdom from God, is a double-edged sword. When you understand that the greatness you possess can be duplicated after any crisis, suicide or hopelessness will not be a thought in your mind.

After Isaac, had been in Gerar for a long time, he sowed in that land, and received in the same year a hundredfold and the Lord blessed him. Isaac waxed great and was very wealthy in that land however; the wells his father's servants had dug in the times of Abraham had been filled with earth. Because he had acquired learned skills and how to hear the voice of the Lord, God was with him and he was able to dig another well in the valley with springing water. Note here that this was a time of famine, and when the herdsmen of Gerar took the well from him, he went to another place and dug a new well but several times, it was taken from him. Because the Lord was with him, Isaac was able to prosper everywhere he went regardless of the opposition he encountered.[393]

The substance of who we are as Christians reside inside us, and no one can take that from us. As Christians, we are not limited by circumstances around us because, the limitless God with all his power dwells in us, and we carry his favor. The supernatural God abide in us and nothing will hinder us in any way. As Christians in these troubled times of uncertainty, we have to learn to hear the voice of God and obey when he gives us instructions.

Prayer

I dwell in this land of the living because "the earth is the Lord's, and everything in it, the world, and all who live in it; for he founded it on

---

393 Genesis 26.

the seas and established it on the waters."³⁹⁴ The earth is created for humans to inhabit, and because I am the beloved of the Lord, I declare that I am blessed in this land of (name of your town) where my feet are planted. "Blessed be the Eternal, my rock. He trains my hands for war, gives me the skills *I need* for battle. *He is* my unfailing love and my citadel. *He is* my tower of strength and my deliverer. He is my shield of protection and my shelter; He holds my people in check under me. Rescue me, and save me from the grasp of these foreigners who speak only lies and don't have truth in their deeds."³⁹⁵

My Father, you have planted my feet upon this land of (name of your town) for your glory. I am a beneficiary of the promise of your Spirit by faith in your Son – Jesus Christ; and I am living by faith in him. He is "the Anointed One, the Liberating King, has redeemed us from the curse of the law by becoming a curse for us. It was stated in the Scriptures, "Everyone who hangs on a tree is cursed by God." This is what God had in mind all along: the blessing He gave to Abraham might extend to all nations through the Anointed One, Jesus; and we are the beneficiaries of this promise of the Spirit that comes only through faith."³⁹⁶ Therefore, I declare that, I am not under any curse but I am blessed and freed by the precious blood of Jesus Christ. I am free from the bondage of destitution and slavery. Free from being a hewer of wood and drawer of water in this land of (name of your town).³⁹⁷ I am free from poverty and mediocrity. I have come to this land of the living to possess my possession to the glory and praise of Jehovah.

My Father, you who made the earth, and formed it, and established it – the LORD is your name. I call unto you this day and as you promised, you will answer and show me your great vastness and

---

394 Psalm 24:1-2 (NIV).
395 Psalm 144:1-2, 11 (VOICE).
396 Galatians 3:12-14 (VOICE).
397 Joshua 9:23.

unsearchable things I do not know. Thank you my Father, for granting me access to inaccessible, unapproachable, and unattainable riches of your glory. My Father, begin to restore health and healing to every aspect of my life and environment, and let me enjoy abundant peace and security in the name of Jesus Christ.[398] My Father, train my ears to hear your voice by your Spirit, train my heart to discern by your Spirit, and train my eyes to see by your Spirit in Jesus name, amen! I apply the blood of Jesus Christ over me and my loved ones for our wholeness in Jesus name.

Prayer of Restoration

Father, I believe in your Son Jesus Christ of Nazareth that you are one with him. I believe your great and mighty works of salvation, deliverance, and liberty. I believe that whatsoever I ask in the name of your Son Jesus Christ, in the lines of who you are and what you are doing; you will bring it to pass so that you will get glory from the Son.[399] Father, send your new wine and rain down on me the former rain and the latter rain of your anointing and glory in the name of Jesus Christ. I pray that all the years, all the blessings, and all that you have destined in my life, that the destructive spirits of the palmerworm have eaten, and the locust have eaten, and the cankerworm have eaten, and the caterpillar have eaten, be restored completely back to me in the name of Jesus Christ of Nazareth. Lord, repay me for all those lost years and restore them back. Lord, remove far from me the spirits of the northern army and drive them into a land barren and desolate, with their face toward the east sea and their back toward the utmost sea in the name of Jesus Christ. And I shall eat in plenty and be satisfied and praise your

---

[398] Jeremiah 33:1-6.
[399] John 14:11-14.

Glorious Name O Lord my God; for you have dealt wondrously with me and I shall never be put to shame.[400]

I begin to declare, from this day forward, every diminishing spirit operating in my life and home is bound in the name of Jesus Christ, and nothing will diminish in my life. From this forward, every spirit of stagnation and limitation operating in my life and home is bound in the name of Jesus Christ. From this day forward, every household demon present in my home is bound in the name of Jesus Christ. From this day forward, every demon that is stunting my spiritual growth is bound in the name of Jesus Christ. I command all the evil spirits that have been bound to depart from me and go to the dry desert where there is no water in the name of Jesus Christ of Nazareth. From this day forward, I will never remain the same. From this day forward, rising higher will remain my only portion. From this day forward, I declare that everything in my life will continue to multiply and increase as I am moving forward, reflecting the glory of the Lord as a mirror; being transformed and metamorphosed into God's image, from His radiance of glory to glory, as the Spirit of the Lord accomplishes this,[401] in the name of Jesus Christ of Nazareth.

My Father, begin to restore my inheritance and all that have been lost back to my lineage and bloodline in the name of Jesus Christ of Nazareth. Thank you Lord for restoration of strength; thank you Lord for restoration of health; thank you Lord for restoration of wealth and resources; thank you Lord for restoration of family and relationships; thank you Lord for restoration of purpose; thank you Lord for restoration of a godly mindset; thank you Lord for restoration of wisdom; and restoration of peace. All these and much more have been restored back to me, and all that the enemy – the thief have stolen from me is being

---

400 Joel 1:4, 2:19-26.
401 2 Corinthians 3:18.

restored sevenfold in the name of Jesus Christ of Nazareth.[402] Father, I thank you for I am flourishing like the palm tree.[403] I thank you Lord, for you have caused me to inherit substance, and have filled my treasures with good things.[404] Elohim, be magnified, for you have pleasure in the prosperity of your servant.[405] No good thing will you withhold from us that walk uprightly.[406]

Lord, thank you for teaching me to profit; and faithfully leading me in the way that I should go.[407] Thank you Lord for your glory is being revealed in my life – and it is shining brighter and brighter. Thank you Lord for my life is brighter than the noonday. Its darkness is like the morning. I have confidence because I have hope.[408] Father, you created all things for your glory. The enemy as a thief came to reap where he did not plant, to steal all that is not his, to kill what he did not create, and to destroy what does not belong to him.[409] All that the enemy has deposited in my body (name), which I am not born with, I command total destruction upon you in the name of Jesus Christ. Every mountain that has stood against the will of God in my life, and every hindrance that has hindered my progress from all sides, I declare that you are coming down for my sake in the name of Jesus Christ.

You evil one, I refuse you to come in to steal, kill, and destroy all that God has given me – it does not belong to you. All that is mine belongs to God and He has blessed me with it - my family, my relationships, my job, my business, my finances, my home, my ministry, and my neighborhood. I serve you notice, you foul spirits, go back to

---

402 Proverbs 6:31.
403 Psalm 92:12.
404 Proverbs 8:21.
405 Psalm 35:27.
406 Psalm 84:11.
407 Isaiah 48:17.
408 Job 11:17-18 (RSV).
409 John 10:10.

your defeated abode; lose your hold from all that concerns me in the name of Jesus Christ of Nazareth who defeated you on the cross of Calvary. God's hedge of protection is upon me and my loved ones, my property and all that concerns me because; I am a tither and a giver.[410]

You foul demons along with your master Satan – a murderer from the beginning, a liar and the father of it,[411] I forbid you to pass over the blood line of Jesus Christ, and serve you notice to leave my blood line alone. The blood of Jesus Christ is against you, the name of Jesus Christ is against you, and I overcome you by the blood of the lamb and the word of my testimony – I am victorious, I am an overcomer, I am the beloved of the Lord, I am a child of the King, I am healed, I am delivered, and I am free.

Satan, I remind you of your defeat and the truth that, you and your hosts of demons have been defeated two thousand years ago, and Jesus Christ, made a public show of you, and triumphed over you in victory.[412] Therefore, you Satan, as lightening fell from heaven; and God my Father, who is LORD over you, has given me the power to tread over you, serpents, and scorpions; and all your wiles and devices have been smashed under my feet. I am triumphantly walking all over the power of the enemy victoriously in the power and authority of the risen Christ Jesus, and nothing shall by any means harm me.[413] Satan, you as the prince of this world has been judged,[414] and I remind you of your imminent future where, you will be cast into the lake of fire and brimstone along with your demons and false prophets, and shall be tormented day and night for all eternity of eternities, world without end, amen![415]

---

410 Malachi 3:10-12.
411 John 8:44.
412 Colossians 2:14-15.
413 Luke 10:18-20.
414 John 16:11.
415 Revelation 20:10.

I refuse to be afraid of those who want to kill my body; they cannot do anymore to me after that. I will rather fear God, who has the power to condemn to hell. He is the one to fear,[416] and I declare that I fear God. "I am not afraid of sudden fear, neither of the desolation of the wicked, when it comes. For the LORD is my confidence, and will keep my foot from being taken."[417] Who then will condemn me? Christ will not because, he is the one who died for us, came back to life again, and now sits at the highest place of honor next to God, interceding for us in heaven. Who or what shall separate me from the love of Christ? Absolutely nothing and no one! Not even tribulation, or distress, or persecution, or famine, or nakedness, or peril, or sword, or any demon in hell. In all these things, I am more than conqueror through him that loved us. I am absolutely and positively confident that nothing whatsoever can separate me from God's love. Neither death nor life, neither angels nor demons, neither my fears for today or worries about tomorrow, not even the powers of hell can separate me from God's love. No power whatsoever in the sky above or in the earth below, absolutely nothing in all creation will ever be able to come between me and the love of God that is revealed in Christ Jesus - my Lord and Master.[418]

Therefore, because of the defeat Satan suffered when Jesus Christ paid the price on the cross of Calvary, I align with all that was accomplished and I declare - I have eternal life, victory, deliverance, a sound mind, healing, and breakthrough. It is not by my power, not by my strength, but by the righteousness and authority of Jesus Christ. I declare that I am victorious over all satanic powers, and I therefore rejoice that my name is written in heaven, and I am heaven bound.[419]

---

416 Luke 12:4-6.
417 Proverbs 3:25-26 (KJV).
418 Romans 8:34-39.
419 Revelation 17:8.

The hour of redemption is here. Lord, I thank you for redeeming all those lost years back to me. I thank you for redeeming lost opportunities and lost relationships. I am the redeemed of the Lord and I thank you Father, for you have redeemed me from the hand of the enemy.[420] All that the enemy has stolen are being redeemed back to me by your Spirit of Power. Just like you gave the children of Israel favor to ask for precious resources from their Egyptian neighbors, that same favor of God is upon my life.[421] I have favor before God and men in Jesus name. Lord, cause men to do good unto me. Everywhere I go, I will not return back empty, for the desire of the righteous shall be granted.[422] Favor follows me, resources of wealth and riches are following me. My home is full of good things because, my trust is in you and verily I shall be fed.[423] I thank you my God, for supplying all my need according to your riches in glory by Christ Jesus my Lord and Savior.[424]

Lord, as I cast my burden upon you, you are sustaining me. You shall never suffer the righteous to be moved.[425] I have more than enough because men are giving unto me and your blessings of abundance is raining down on me. You O Lord satisfy my mouth with good things and with the bread of heaven, so that my youth is renewed like the eagles.[426] Blessed be the Lord, who daily loads me with benefits, even the God of my salvation.[427] I have enough resources to support and advance the kingdom of God on earth. I rejoice in the LORD; I will joy in the God of my salvation. YHWH Adonai (The LORD God) is my strength,

---

420 Psalm 107:2.
421 Exodus 11:2-3, 3:21-22.
422 Proverbs 10:24.
423 Psalm 37:3.
424 Philippians 4:19.
425 Psalm 55:22.
426 Psalm 103:5, 105:40.
427 Psalm 68:19.

and He will make my feet like hinds' feet, and He will make me to walk upon mine high places in Jesus Christ name, amen![428] I apply the blood of Jesus Christ over me and my loved ones for our wholeness in Jesus name.

INCREASE

PRAYER

My Father, begin to enlarge the place of my tent, and increase me in every direction to fill the world for your glory. I declare that my offspring will take over the nations and revitalize long-abandoned towns for the glory and praise of your Holy name.[429] I thank you Lord that you have accelerated and catapulted me to where you have ordained me to be in this season right now in the name of Jesus Christ. Thank you Lord because, divine connection to yield overnight reside in my life. Just like Aaron's rod which sprouted, budded, blossomed, and produced almonds in one day,[430] likewise, you have restored to me everything suddenly in the name of Jesus Christ of Nazareth.

Father, I thank you, as you have declared the end from the beginning, and have declared how things will end, your intentions will surely manifest in my life.[431] My Father, you dwell in me with all your power and anointing. I am all that you are inside of me. Your end for me is good and blessed. I am victorious; I am an overcomer; I have abundance of grace and mercy; I have more than enough. All that I need is already provided for. I can do all things through Christ who has given me the

---

428 Habakkuk 3:19.
429 Isaiah 54:2-3.
430 Numbers 17:8.
431 Isaiah 46:9-10.

strength.[432] I am healed, saved, and delivered. I am prosperous and I have the Shalom – peace of God. I am increasing from all sides. I have God's favor of wealth upon my life. The Spirit of the Lord is upon me to preach the good news that, I am the beloved of God, I am in Christ, and I am loved. The good news is the revelation of the Messiah - Jesus Christ. I am preaching the good news declaring that the kingdom of heaven is at hand, with signs and wonders following – healing the sick, cleansing lepers, raising the dead, and casting out demons. Freely I have received, freely will I give.[433] Jesus Christ came to bring hope to the hopeless, peace, liberty, salvation, justice, and freedom; to set the captives free, to break Satanic chains of bondage from peoples' lives, and to declare the hope of eternity with God – this is the good news of the gospel. I believe that I will be with you Jesus where you are, that I may behold your glory.[434]

My father and my God, cause me to live in safety and be my God. Give me singleness of heart and action so that I will always fear you for my own good and the good of my children after me. My God, never stop doing good to me. Inspire me to fear you oh Lord, never to turn away from you. O Lord, I thank you for you rejoice in doing good to me. Father, give me all the prosperity you have promised me for the work of the gospel. Father, cause me to sign deeds as you begin to restore my fortunes through the purchases of fields, lands, houses, and businesses for the work of the ministry, in the name of Jesus Christ.[435] I apply the blood of Jesus Christ over me and my loved ones for our wholeness in Jesus name.

---

432 Philippians 4:13.
433 Matthew 10:7-8.
434 John 17:24.
435 Jeremiah 32:37-44.

Ministry Supporters

Prayer

Father, I ask you to give me the heathen for my inheritance, and the uttermost parts of the earth for my possession for the sake of the kingdom in Jesus name.[436] I thank you for sending ministry partners and supporters that you have ordained to partner with me in this work of the kingdom; who will support me both spiritually and with their resources for the vision you have given me in expanding your kingdom in this world. Just like Joshua with his team had victory for the children of Israel when Aaron and Hur held the hands of Moses in unity;[437] likewise, these ministry supporters you are sending, would help and support me to carry out the vision you have established in my life.

Father, wherever they are, I declare that they will locate me speedily in the name of Jesus Christ. Father, open their ears and hearts to hear your voice to know that we are working together in unity to carry out the message of the truth of your Word in advancing your kingdom on earth; and soften their hearts to do good unto me. Thank you Father that these ministry supporters are here and I bless them with the blessing of The Most High God. Lord, I thank you for given them eyes to see, ears to hear, and a heart to know and understand their role in my life and ministry.

God of our Lord Jesus the Anointed, Father of Glory: I call out to you on behalf of your people (those who support the work of the ministry). Give them minds ready to receive wisdom and revelation so they will truly know you. Open the eyes of their hearts, and let the light of your truth flood in. Shine your light on the hope you are calling them

---

436 Psalm 2:8.
437 Exodus 17:9-13.

to embrace. Reveal to them the glorious riches you are preparing as their inheritance. Let them see the full extent of your power that is at work in those of us who believe, and may it be done according to your power and might"[438] in Jesus name, amen.

I command every spiritual seed-eaten palmerworm, locust, cankerworm, and caterpillar to be totally destroyed with the fire of the Holy Ghost in the lives of those who are partnering with me in the work of our Master Jesus Christ. Lord, cause your face to shine upon them. Be gracious unto them and grant them your peace – Shalom. "O Lord, thou art my God; I will exalt thee, I will praise thy name; for thou hast done wonderful things; thy counsels of old are faithfulness and truth."[439] I plead and apply the blood of Jesus Christ over the ministry supporters in Jesus name.

Ah, Sovereign Lord, you have made the heavens and the earth by your great power and outstretched arm. Nothing is too hard for you. You show love to thousands but bring the punishment for the parents' sins into the laps of their children after them. Great and mighty God, whose name is the Lord Almighty, great are your purposes and mighty are your deeds, your eyes are open to the ways of all mankind; you reward each person according to their conduct and as their deeds deserve. You performed signs and wonders in Egypt and have continued them to this day in Israel and among all mankind, and have gained the renown that is still yours. You brought your people Israel out of Egypt with signs and wonders, by a mighty hand and an outstretched arm and with great terror.[440]

---

438 Ephesians 1:17-19 (VOICE).
439 Isaiah 25:1.
440 Jeremiah 32:17-21 (NIV).

Holy Spirit

God promised that He will never leave us nor forsake us; and I have this confidence, the Lord is my helper, I will not be afraid what man will do unto me.[441] The hope we have is that the Holy Spirit will never leave us, and God's angels are always around to watch over us.[442] It is so comforting to know that my Father in heaven, did not leave us comfortless. All the comfort we need, we have it in the person of the Holy Spirit who is our comforter, advocate, intercessor, counselor, strengthener, and standby; all the knowledge we need, we have it in the person of the Holy Spirit who is our teacher, and will teach us all things; all the mysteries and answers we are searching for, we have it in the person of the Holy Spirit who is the revealer of secrets; when we need to remember all that God has told us, we have the Holy Spirit who will remind us of everything that God has spoken in His Word through His Son – Jesus Christ.[443]

As Christians, we cannot operate in the power of God with signs and wonders following without the Holy Spirit. We have to totally depend on the Holy Spirit to guide us in everything we do for the kingdom of God. In order to experience the supernatural in our speech and preaching, it has to be by the demonstration of the Spirit and power.[444] The Holy Spirit enables us in prayer, he revives us in prayer, and baptize us with fire that we need to be effective in the kingdom of God, all through prayer.

---

441 Hebrews 13:4-6
442 Psalm 91:11.
443 John 14:26 (AMP).
444 1 Corinthians 2:3-5.

Prayer

I worship and give you praise Holy Spirit of The Most High God. You are worthy of my praise. I honor and lift you up my comforter, teacher and reminder of all things. You will never leave me nor forsake me, and will be with me forever. You will continue to lead me and in your power, I will move and declare the righteousness of God on this earth. It is in the demonstration of your power I will preach the gospel of salvation to the dying world,[445] for the kingdom of God is not in word, but in power.[446]

My Father, I believe in your Holy Spirit and acknowledge that He lives in me as my comforter, teacher, revealer of secrets, reminder of all things, and much more.[447] My steps are ordered and directed by your Spirit, I walk in your Spirit, I am filled with your Spirit, my mouth is filled with your Spirit, my mind is filled with your Spirit, and I pray through and by the Holy Spirit. Holy Spirit, I voluntarily yield my spirit, soul, and body unto you to control, dominate, rule, and use as you choose. I choose to yield myself, my will, my emotion, and thoughts for your glory to use as you choose. I willingly submit myself absolutely in surrender for your glory. I thank you Father, for filling me to the fullest of your Holy Spirit. Holy Spirit, I totally and completely yield myself to you in surrender and obedience.

Holy Spirit, move as you will in my life; purge me and demonstrate your power and glory in my life; demonstrate your anointing through me as a vessel unto honor, sanctified, and consecrated, useful and ready for any good work, unto our Master's noble use.[448] Holy Spirit, you are Holy, you are worthy, I worship you, and I acknowledge that you are God. You are worthy indeed of my praise. I wor-

---

445 1 Corinthians 2:4.
446 1 Corinthians 4:20.
447 John 14:26.
448 2 Timothy 2:20-22.

ship you Elohim; I give you all the praise, glory, honor, adoration, majesty, dominion, authority, and power; and I ascribe greatness to your Holiness, Amen!

Write down your Testimony and Answers to Prayers

CHAPTER 5

Ungodly Covenants

Thinking "generational" is so important because, it is your lifeline. What are you passing on to your bloodline?

~ JOSEPHINE AKHAGBEME

THE DEVIL'S PURPOSE AND MISSION is to steal, kill, and destroy all that God has blessed us with. But the good news is that Christ came to give us abundant life.[449] The devil begins his destructive agenda early in a person's life. Most times, it begins from past generations. He thrives in the ignorance of the next generation and continues his destructive agenda as long as he is allowed. Ignorance is one of the tools of the devil in the life of a believer. This is why the scripture says "my people are destroyed for lack of knowledge."[450] You may have heard of this saying "what I don't know won't hurt me." This is a lie and the truth is that, it will eventually hurt that person either directly or indirectly. It is important to get as much information as possible about your family tree. This will help you to be specific in breaking curses from your life and bloodline forever. Even if you don't know, it is necessary to break all curses you can

---
449 John 10:10.
450 Hosea 4:6.

think of. In doing this, you have nothing to lose but everything to gain if per adventure, such curses were present in your lineage.

God has set before you this day a blessing and a curse; A blessing, if you obey the commandments of the LORD your God, and a curse, if you will not obey the commandments of the LORD your God.[451] God has equally set before you, life and death, blessing and cursing: therefore, he encourages you to choose life that you and thy seed may live.[452] It is evident from this passage that blessing and cursing does not end with your generation; it passes on to the next generation. In breaking curses from your life, you are not only doing yourself much good, but your entire bloodline for ever will benefit from your choice to be set free. A lot of people are suffering today because of the curses that were passed down to them from their parents and forefathers.

The devil started this strategic multi-level destructive agenda from the beginning of humanity. He started way back at the garden when he succeeded in deceiving Adam and Eve in disobeying God's commandment not to eat from the forbidden tree. He did not wait to tempt them after they had children rather; he understood that if he can succeed in deceiving them into disobedience, he can contaminate the entire human race once and for all. This is the same strategy he is using on people today. His plan is to place a curse on one of the parents, and he will continue to destroy that lineage for several generations to come. The story does not end there, the good news is that Jesus Christ also understood this spiritual law and in like mindedness, He came with a purpose to destroy all the works of the devil[453] - once and for all. He successfully accomplished this when He died and rose again and declared "all power is given unto me in heaven and in earth."[454] And

---

451 Deuteronomy 11:26-38.
452 Deuteronomy 30:19.
453 1 John 3:8.
454 Matthew 28:18.

before He went back to heaven, He handed to the church (you and me) the power to tread on serpents and scorpions, and over all the power of the enemy: and nothing shall by any means hurt us.[455]

Jesus said: these signs and wonders shall follow them that believe; in my name (Jesus) shall they cast out devils (demons); they shall speak with new tongues; they shall take up serpents; and if they drink any deadly thing, it shall not hurt them; they shall lay hands on the sick, and they shall recover.[456] God Almighty, conferred on us the power (authority) to accomplish all these successfully in the name of His Son – Jesus Christ. The name of Jesus Christ is the only name that carry the miraculous power and authority of God Almighty with signs and wonders following. Because of the humility and obedience of Jesus unto death of the cross, "God exalted him to the highest place and gave him the name that is above every name, that at the name of Jesus every knee should bow, in heaven and on earth and under the earth, and every tongue acknowledge that Jesus Christ is Lord, to the glory of God the Father."[457]

As a Christian, these signs are part of the promises Christ gave us. We ought to exercise our belief in faith to operate in the supernatural with signs and wonders following. This people, is the victorious end of the story. Generational curses are transferable to the third and fourth generation;[458] while God's blessings follow a blood line unto a thousand generations.[459] The good news is that; it is possible to break free from these curses by the power of God. Satan and his demons are defeated already amen!

---

455 Luke 10:19.
456 Mark 16:17-18.
457 Philippians 2:9-11 (NIV).
458 Exodus 20:5, 34:7.
459 Deuteronomy 7:9.

Prayer

My Father, I come to your throne of holiness by the blood of Jesus Christ. I ask your Holy Spirit to enable and empower me to pray. I ask you my Father, to raise a standard against the enemy on my behalf as I pray. I thank you for your forgiveness and mercy. I thank you Father, for purifying me from the pollution of all the bad things I have done.[460] Father, in any way I may have given the enemy a legal ground to torment and afflict me through curses, that may have resulted in sickness, disease, unforgiveness, anger, fear, shame, mental illness, or marital problems, I ask that you would destroy these strongholds in my life in the name of Jesus Christ.

Father, begin to destroy all spoken and unspoken curses that have been released over my life; and all inner vows I may have made in the name of Jesus Christ. For how can anyone put a curse upon me whom God has not cursed? Or damn me whom God has not damned? I declare that I am blessed of God and no one can curse me. I cover myself with the blood of Jesus Christ. I also plead the blood of Jesus Christ over my loved ones. I cover my home and property with the blood of Jesus Christ. Father, as I pray these prayers, saturate this atmosphere with your presence in the name of Jesus Christ.

Father, as your blessed child, I ask you in the name of Jesus Christ to destroy all the curses of the enemy from my life, and begin to reverse them to blessings. Father, I thank you for I am your honorable vessel, sanctified and consecrated for special purposes, made holy and prepared to do your good work my Master.[461] I thank you Father, for I am the righteousness of God in Christ Jesus.[462] My Father – The Eternal, you are my war club and weapon for battle; and with you, I will smash

---
460 1 John 1:9.
461 2 Timothy 2:21.
462 Romans 3:22.

and destroy ungodliness and wicked kingdoms,[463] not by my power or strength, but by your Spirit. I thank you for giving me your glory of authority and protection from every assault of the enemy to crush them. As I walk among serpents and scorpions, nothing shall injure me, and no one can put a hand on me without your permission [464] because, the battle belongs to the Lord and the victory is mine.[465]

I am born of God and overcome the world by the power of the Holy Spirit. This is the victory that overcomes the world. The wicked one cannot touch me because I am covered in the blood of Jesus Christ.[466] Father, I thank you for your overwhelming victory is mine through Christ, who loves me.[467] Father, I thank you for you always cause me to triumph, using me to spread the knowledge of Christ everywhere like a sweet perfume.[468] Lord, I thank you for you have given unto me the power and authority to trample upon serpents and scorpions (including his physical and mental strength and ability), and over all the power the enemy possesses, and nothing shall in any way harm me in Jesus name.[469] Lord, I thank you for removing your hand of judgment against me and dispersing the armies of my enemies far from me. You are the LORD, the true King of Israel, the Eternal One, and you are standing right here by my side; therefore, I have no reason to be afraid ever again.[470]

Father, as I pray these prayers by the empowerment of your Holy Spirit, I understand that we may be in the flesh, but we are not waging war according to the flesh. For the weapons of our warfare are not

---

463 Jeremiah 51:20.
464 Luke 10:19.
465 1 Samuel 17:47.
466 1 John 5:4, 18.
467 Romans 8:37.
468 2 Corinthians 2:14 (NLT).
469 Luke 10:19 (AMP).
470 Zephaniah 3:15 (VOICE).

of the flesh but have divine power to destroy strongholds, arguments, and every loft opinion raised against the knowledge of God, and taking every thought captive in obedience to Christ.[471]

I understand that Satan and his demons are defeated already, and he is operating from a defeated platform in the beginning of the story. In lightning speed, he was cast out of heaven.[472] Therefore, in the power of the Holy Spirit, I declare my victorious end of the story over all the machinations of the enemy in my life in the name of Jesus Christ. I am declaring from a higher victorious realm of authority, and begin to cancel every ungodly covenant in my life, every ungodly covenant in my marriage, every ungodly covenant in my children's lives, and every ungodly covenant in my home. I renounce every involvement with witchcraft and the occult knowingly or through dreams, in the name of Jesus Christ of Nazareth. Every ungodly compact or agreement that has held me bound, I begin to speak to you - hear the Word of the Lord and lose your hold from my life in the name of Jesus Christ of Nazareth. Thank you, Lord, I give you all the praise and glory, amen!

Father, I take refuge in you - my Lord than to trust in humans or princes. Behold, Satan and his demons surround me, but in the name of the LORD I cut them down. They surround me on every side, but in the name of the LORD I cut them down. They swarmed around me like bees, but they are consumed as quickly as burning thorns; in the name of the LORD I cut them down. I am pushed back and about to fall, but the LORD is my helper. The LORD is my strength and my defense; he is my salvation.[473] I apply the blood of Jesus Christ over me and my loved ones for our wholeness in Jesus name.

---

471 2 Corinthians 10:3-5 (ESV).
472 Luke 10:18.
473 Psalm 118:8-14 (NIV).

Prayer against Evil Pronouncements

As Christians, we are confronted with spiritual battle every moment. But the good news is that, the creative power and ability of God to change our circumstances and situation dwells in all believers. Therefore, as believers, we have been given the overcoming enablement to withstand the onslaught of satanic attacks against us. Jesus Christ established for us the victory way ahead of the battle. Victory is guaranteed every step of the spiritual battle we encounter in our walk with the Lord. Though sometimes, we feel the pain and the sting of the spiritual warfare we encounter, but the good news is that "we know [with great confidence] that God [who is deeply concerned about us] causes all things to work together [as a plan] for good for those who love God, to those who are called according to His plan *and* purpose."[474]

Prayer

All decrees, declarations, pronouncements, curses, agreements, covenants, conclusions and results, that have been made in the spiritual realm against me, against my home, against my finances, against my children, and against my marriage, hear the Word of the Lord. I break all agreements with hell over my life, over my dwelling place, over my ministry, over my home, over my children's lives, over my finances, over my purpose, and over my destiny. God has set me over the nations and over the kingdoms therefore, I begin to root out and pull down, and destroy and throw down[475] all the evil machinations of the enemy and all his curses from my life and the lives of my loved ones in the name of Jesus Christ.

---

474 Romans 8:28 (AMP).
475 Jeremiah 1:10.

I break all these ungodly agreements and covenants in the name of Jesus Christ of Nazareth.[476] I declare, you will not stand; you will not stay; and you will not take root in the soil of my heart. I forbid you to take a strong hold in my life. I forbid you to be planted in my home, in the name of Jesus Christ of Nazareth. I curse every ungodly relationship that is trying to resurrect in my life through dreams. May the Lord cause you to be totally destroyed and annihilated, in the name of Jesus Christ. I sever every ungodly bond that has been established in my life from the past. I command you by the power of the Holy Spirit to be uprooted and destroyed. I break your yoke, I break your bondage, and I break your hold from my life, in the name of Jesus Christ of Nazareth.

Father, begin to break from my life all spiritual chains of stagnation and limitation that have been placed upon me in the name of Jesus Christ. Father, release your destroying fire to melt all those chains right now in the name of Jesus Christ. All bondage of shame that have been placed upon my life, by the authority of Jehovah God, I command you to be removed from my life forever in the name of Jesus Christ. I declare that, shame will never be my portion in the name of Jesus Christ. Father, I thank you for releasing your angels with two-edged swords of fire, standing guard over me.

All ungodly agreements with hell, all ungodly agreements with the grave, and all ungodly agreements with death, I refuse you entrance into my life and my lineage either through dreams or otherwise. The Lord has caused me to come up out of every grave the enemy have dug for me in the name of Jesus Christ.[477] I renounce and break free from all those ungodly satanic covenants that have been entered into with idols, false gods, and demons, on my behalf by my bloodline or lineage, my ancestors or forefathers, or by any member of my family and my husband's family. I renounce and break free by the help of the Holy

---

476 Isaiah 28:18.
477 Ezekiel 37:12.

Ghost from all unholy oats, unholy covenant, ungodly decrees, ungodly proclamations, and ungodly results which I have declared from my lips, or entered into knowingly or unknowingly in the name of Jesus Christ of Nazareth.[478]

I cancel all ungodly and unholy incantations and pronouncements against my life. I release the fire of the Holy Ghost to burn and destroy your powers over my life in the name of Jesus Christ. I command you to cease your manipulations in my life and mind. I dismantle you and forbid you to come into my life; and I denounce and reject you. I free myself from your yoke of condemnation and regret; I uproot you from my bloodline, from my home, from my children's lives, from my finances, from my destiny by the power of the Holy Ghost. Only the covenant with God Almighty, the creator of the universe, the Father of our Lord Jesus Christ, and my Abba - Father will stand in the name of Jesus Christ of Nazareth. I apply the blood of Jesus Christ over me and my loved ones for our wholeness in Jesus name.

CURSES

Iniquity is premeditated and habitual sin. One interesting truth about iniquity is that, it is transferable up to the fourth generation, depending on when the curses originally started. In other words, a father or mother's iniquity carries into the third and fourth generation.[479] In order to stop the cycle, someone in that bloodline will have to break the curse. The opposite of a curse is blessing. God's covenant and mercy upon a believer passes on to a thousand generations.[480] God, who is aware of these implications, set before us life and death, blessing and cursing. He encourages us to choose life that we and our seed (blood-

---

478 Exodus 23:32.
479 Exodus 20:5; 34:7, Numbers 14:18.
480 Deuteronomy 7:9.

line) may live.[481] The good news about curses is that, Christ has broken them from our lives and we do not have to suffer the consequences any longer. He redeemed us from the curse of the law, being made a curse for us: for it is written, cursed is everyone that hangs on a tree.[482]

The Greek word for *cursed* is *epikataratos*. This word is related to the Greek word *epi* which means, Christ took our curses, carried them upon himself, bore them, covered them, died for them, was made guilty, and overcame for us. This word is also related to the Greek word *kata*, whose actions of carrying the curses upon himself deserved a death penalty. In obedience to the requirement of assuming these curses, Jesus died for us on the cross of Calvary. This word is further related to the Greek word *katara*. Jesus was accursed – being made a curse for us in order that we may be blessed.[xvi]

It is important to note that people who hate God are cursed.[483] But as a child of God, an undeserved curse will not rest upon you. No curse for any reason will come upon you.[484] There is always a cause for any curse. There are curses of all sorts that come upon an individual and these may include: *word curses, inner vows, ancestral and generational curses, territorial curses (linked to territories), racial curses (linked to race), curses due to sins, transgressions, habits, or addictions, to name but a few. Additionally, there are also root spirits linked to curses that the enemy uses as a legal ground in a person's life to oppress that individual. These are known as root spirits of infirmity, divination, fear, bondage, whoredom, idolatry, haughtiness, perverseness, antichrist, deaf and dumb, heaviness, lying, jealousy, error, and slumber or sleep* (Dr. Malone, 2011, pp. 125-134).[xvii]

---

481 Deuteronomy 30:19.
482 Galatians 3:11-14.
483 Exodus 20:5, Deuteronomy 28:15, Proverbs 3:33, John 7:49, Galatians 3:10.
484 Proverbs 26:2.

Prayer to Cancel Curses

My Father, I thank you for your word of truth that has been revealed to me. I acknowledge that I don't have to carry all these curses because; Jesus Christ already paid the price and carried them for me. I repent of all my sins. Forgive my sin of (name sins). I repent and turnaround from them right now. I renounce all involvement with the occult, witchcraft, and all satanic activities I may have been involved with knowingly or unknowingly. I renounce all allegiance to Satan and his wicked demons. Jesus, I ask you to come into my life, be my Lord and Master. Empower me by your Holy Spirit from this moment forward. I thank you for your forgiveness and mercy upon my life.

My Father, based on your power in my life to tread on serpents and scorpions, and over all the powers of the enemy, nothing shall hurt me.[485] Therefore, I begin to break all curses from my lineage and bloodline that has been passed down unto me generationally, or through my ancestors in the name of Jesus Christ. I break from my life all curses that are linked to me in any way in the name of Jesus Christ. I break their hold from my life right now and forbid them to pass on in the name of Jesus Christ. I command all curses, in any form or fashion in my life that are operational or dormant to be uprooted from me and my bloodline in the name of Jesus Christ.

I break the yoke of sickness curses of (name sickness) from my life in the name of Jesus Christ. I break free from all generational and ancestral curses of (name known curses) from my life in the name of Jesus Christ. I break the curses of racial identity from my life in the name of Jesus Christ. I break the curses of territorial affiliation from my life in the name of Jesus Christ. I break the curses of national identity from my life in the name of Jesus Christ. I break all curses of racism and/or tribalism from my life in the name of Jesus Christ. I break free from all word curses spoken over my life and all inner vows I have made or

---
485 Luke 10:19.

entered into knowingly or unknowingly in the name of Jesus Christ. I uproot from my life and bloodline all curses that are present in the name of Jesus Christ. By the virtue of the blood of Jesus Christ, I am free from all curses. Jesus took my pain, bore my suffering, was pierced for my transgressions, and was crushed for my iniquities. The punishment that procured my peace was on him, and by his wounds I am healed, saved, and delivered.[486]

I command all symptoms associated to all curses in my life to begin to bow before my Lord and Savior Jesus Christ. My Father, send your fire to burn all symptoms associated to all curses in my life in the name of Jesus. I uproot these spirits connected to the symptoms and I break their hold from my life, and send them to dry places never to return back to me in the name of Jesus Christ. Any stubborn spirit left, I release the hornet of the Holy Spirit and dismantle your hold from my life right now, and I send you to dry places without water in the name of Jesus Christ.

My Father, I thank you for your deliverance, and I ask you to fill all empty areas in my life with your Holy Spirit. Fill me afresh with the breath of heaven. Fill me with your presence and glory. Cause your blood to shield me and my bloodline from all satanic attacks in Jesus name. Thank you for deliverance has come to my household, amen! I apply the blood of Jesus Christ over me and my loved ones for our wholeness in Jesus name.

Prayer against Unclean Spirits

Holy Spirit, I ask you to pray through me for I do not know how. Help me to articulate these prayers that are being offered with groaning too profound for words. My Father, you pursue and explore the human heart intimately and know the Spirit's mind because He pleads to God

---
[486] Isaiah 53.

on my behalf to align my life with your Will. I am therefore confident, that God is able to orchestrate everything to work toward something good and beautiful because I love Him and accept His invitation to live according to His plan. Therefore, because God is on my side, I will not fear anything or anyone.[487]

I begin to command all unholy and unclean spirits to stop following and tormenting me, or influencing me through others. By the power of the Almighty God, I bind and break free from the root spirits of infirmity, divination, fear, bondage, whoredom, idolatry, haughtiness, perverseness, antichrist, deaf and dumb, heaviness, lying, jealousy, error, and slumber/sleep in the name of Jesus Christ. I come against every spirit of (name known spirits in your family tree) madness and mental illness from my family tree; I bind all sickness spirits linked to Alzheimer's disease, diabetes, and high blood pressure, that are attached to my family tree; I bind the spirit of stubbornness from my family tree; I bind the spirit of suicide and hopelessness from my family tree; I bind the spirit of death and abortion from my family tree; I bind the spirit of divorce from my family tree; I bind the spirit of sexual promiscuity from my family tree; and I bind the spirit of polygamy from my family tree, I bind the wicked spirits of Jezebel and Ahab from my life and family tree in the name of Jesus Christ of Nazareth. I command all these spirits that have been bound to depart from me right now and go into dry waterless places in the name of Jesus Christ. Just like Jesus Christ cursed the fig tree to wither and die from the root and it was so[488] likewise, I command every spiritual root curses present in my life and bloodline to die and wither, and be uprooted from my life in the name of Jesus Christ.

I plead the blood of Jesus Christ over me and my bloodline, and forbid all curses from passing over to my blood line (my children and

---

[487] Romans 8:25-31.
[488] Mark 11:4.

grandchildren). I forbid their manifestations in any of my generations from now onward and forever in the name of Jesus Christ. Surely, no curse or sorcery can touch me, and no magic has any power against me in the name of Jesus Christ.[489] Every ungodly pronouncement over my household will not prosper in the name of Jesus Christ. I command you right now to depart from my presence forever. All unholy and unclean spirits that has tormented my children and home in any way or capacity, I command you right now to desist from following us, or harassing us and influencing our thoughts[490] in the name of Jesus Christ of Nazareth.

The Lord rebuke you Satan along with your hosts of demons; the blood of Jesus Christ is against you. Lord, begin to raise a standard against the enemy on my behalf right now in the name of Jesus Christ of Nazareth.[491] The Lord shall cause the enemies who rise up against me to be defeated before me. When they shall come out against me one way, they will flee before me seven different ways in confusion, in the name of Jesus Christ.[492] God is keeping me in His perfect peace as I put my trust in Him, because my thoughts are often on you my Lord.[493] Thank You my Father for Your authority. I thank You for Your power and empowerment; and I thank You for Your Holy Spirit. I thank You because, I am an overcomer - for greater is He that is in me, than he that is in the world.[494]

Father, I thank you for the victory you have wrought in my life today. You are God above all gods. There is none powerful than you are. Every knee will bow before you my Master, and every tongue will

---

489 Numbers 23:23.
490 Matthew 8:16-17.
491 Isaiah 59:19.
492 Deuteronomy 28:7.
493 Isaiah 26:3.
494 1 John 4:4.

confess that Jesus Christ is Lord, to the glory of God the Father.[495] Right now, I bow my knees before Your Majesty in submission to your authority. I confess that You Elohim are the true God Eternal. All power in heaven and earth are yours my King.[496]

Father, I thank you for the blood of Jesus Christ which procured my freedom, forgiveness and peace with God. Christ who existed before God made anything at all is the exact likeness of the unseen God. Christ himself is the Creator who made everything in heaven and earth, the things we can see and the things we can't; the spirit world with its kings and kingdoms, its rulers and authorities; all were made by Christ for his own use and glory. He was before all else began and it is his power that holds everything together. He is the Head of the body made up of his people—that is, his Church—which he began; and he is the Leader of all those who arise from the dead, so that he is first in everything; for God wanted all of Himself to be in his Son – Jesus Christ.[497] Father, you created the destroyer, and you have made a way of escape for us. Thank you, Elohim, you created all things for your glory. Thank you for the victory I have in you. Thank you Lord for who you are - The Great God Eternal! I apply the blood of Jesus Christ over me and my loved ones for our wholeness in Jesus name.

THANKSGIVING

Father, I thank you for deliverance from generational curses and ungodly covenants. Thank you for fighting my battle and establishing the victory way ahead of the battle. Thank you for your power that dismantled all the powers of the enemy on my behalf. Thank you for given me the power to overcome the enemy and nothing shall by any means

---

495 Philippians 2:11.
496 Matthew 28:18.
497 Colossians 1:16 (TLB).

hurt me.⁴⁹⁸ Thank you for I am saved, healed, and delivered. Thank you for the victory you established for me on the cross of Calvary. Thank you my Father, for greater is He that lives in me, than he that is in the world.⁴⁹⁹ That same power – the Spirit of God, which raised Jesus Christ from the death, dwells in me; and He that raised Christ from the dead will continue to give life to my mortal body through His Spirit who dwells in me.⁵⁰⁰ Father, I thank you for you have made me alive in Christ. It is by your grace that I am saved. God has raised me up with Christ and I sit with Him in heavenly realms in order that in the coming ages, he might shew the incomparable riches of his grace, expressed in his kindness to me in Christ Jesus,⁵⁰¹ amen!

Father, I thank you for exposing the enemy – the devil. He was a murderer from the beginning, and there is no truth in him. When he speaks, he speaks lies – his native tongue; for he is a liar, and the father of it.⁵⁰² He is also a thief who has come to steal, and to kill, and to destroy. But the good news is that you my Lord, have destroyed the effectiveness of the devil's power and have come to give me life more abundantly. You are the door and if any one enters in, he shall be saved. You are the good shepherd, and you as the good shepherd have given your life for the sheep – your church.⁵⁰³

Lord I thank you for your Word will not return unto you void. For just as the rain and snow come down from heaven, and do not return there without watering the earth, making it bring forth and sprout, yielding seed for the sower and bread for eating, so will your word be that goes out of your mouth – it won't return to you empty. Instead, it

---

498 Luke 10:19.
499 1 John 4:4.
500 Romans 8:11.
501 Ephesians 2:5-7 (NIV).
502 John 8:44.
503 John 10:9-11.

will accomplish what you desire, and achieve the purpose for which you sent it.[504] You are watching over your Word to perform it, and none of your Word will fall to the ground concerning my life in the name of Jesus Christ,[505] amen!

Who shall separate us from the love of Christ? *Shall* tribulation, or distress, or persecution, or famine, or nakedness, or peril, or sword? As it is written "For Your sake we are killed all day long; We are accounted as sheep for the slaughter" Yet in all these things we are more than conquerors through Him who loved us. For I am persuaded that neither death nor life, nor angels nor principalities nor powers, nor things present nor things to come, nor height nor depth, nor any other created thing, shall be able to separate me from the love of God which is in Christ Jesus our Lord.[506] I apply the blood of Jesus Christ over me and my loved ones for our wholeness in Jesus name.

I Have the Mind of Christ

I declare that I possess the mind of Christ because I walk by the Spirit and I am spiritually alive. I have the ability to discern and apply what the Holy Spirit reveals to me. I am daily guided by the thoughts and purposes of Christ; and I am not subject to human judgments.[507] I have eyes to see, ears to hear, and a heart to know God's truth. I am living in accordance with the Spirit and have my mind set on what the Spirit desires. My mind is governed by the Spirit and I have life and peace. I submit to God's authority and please Him with my lifestyle.[508] Therefore, I forbid any negative identity that is trying to manifest in my

---

504 Isaiah 55:10-11 (ISV).
505 Exodus 18:18, 1 Samuel 3:19.
506 Romans 8:35-39 (NKJV).
507 1 Corinthians 2:15-16.
508 Romans 8:4-8.

life. I begin to apply the blood of Jesus Christ over my mind, over my bloodline, over my generation, over my lineage, and over my children and their seed forever in the name of Jesus Christ. I declare that I am a new creature in Christ Jesus; old things are passed away behold, all things have become new in my life from this day forward.[509] I declare that my mind is stayed on God and because I trust in Him, I have perfect peace – Shalom of God.[510] I declare that, I am the righteousness of God in Christ Jesus, amen!

ELOHIM

I thank you Father, that by your Holy Spirit, I am guarding my heart with all diligence and alertness.[511] I thank you Father, for I have your wisdom, knowledge, and understanding. I thank you for I have the mind of Christ,[512] and I have clarity. Holy Spirit of God, you are my comforter, my teacher, and reminder of all things.[513] I thank you for being with me, and empowering me for the work of the gospel. I thank you Father, for in Jesus Christ I am blessed. In Jesus Christ, I have abundant life. in Jesus Christ, I am saved and delivered. In Jesus Christ, I am free from the curse associated with the fall of humanity. In Jesus Christ, I have all that I need for life and godliness. In Jesus Christ, my children and their children are blessed forever. In Jesus Christ, I am increasing from all sides. In Jesus Christ, I am wealthy and spiritually alive. In Jesus Christ, I live and move and have my being.[514] In Jesus Christ no curse or enchantment against me and my

---

509 Matthew 8:16-17.
510 Isaiah 26:3.
511 Proverbs 4:23.
512 1 Corinthians 2:16.
513 John 14:24-26.
514 Acts 17:28.

loved ones will prosper. In Jesus Christ, I am wise and prudent. In Jesus Christ, I will resurrect after death; I have life eternal and my name is written in the book of life.[515]

---

515 Revelation 13:8.

Write down your Testimony and Answers to Prayers

NOTES

Introduction
    Pray constantly in faith and belief, always giving thanks.
    Be quick to offer forgiveness.
    Be careful about the words you speak. Always speak positive words in alignment with the word of God.
    Be a humble and available vessel to be used by God.
    Always pray in the name of Jesus Christ.
    Guard your heart, thoughts, and emotion against the enemy's suggestions.
    Constantly counter the lies of Satan with the word of God.
    Think on things that are true, honest, just, pure, lovely, and of good report.
    Constantly engage a proactive and intentional process of audible declaration of God's word over any situation and circumstances you encounter.
    Desire to do more for the kingdom of God here on earth as his faithful laborer.
    Approach God in prayer with a settled belief.
    Do not entertain unbelief, faithlessness, doubt, fear, or anxiety when you are faced with the trials of life.
    Be aware of your victorious position in Christ.

Chapter 1

All that you need for life and godliness is in existence already, and has been given to all believers in Christ Jesus.

Having a settled belief in your heart produces confidence and boldness to come into God's presence.

Recognize that our battle is not against other humans, but it is against the devil and his demons.

Chapter 2

As a Christian, you have been given the power and authority over Satan and his demons; start utilizing your authority against his wicked agenda on earth.

Anything that does not align with the word of God is a lie.

The finished work of Calvary includes: healing, wholeness, peace, joy, salvation, freedom, liberty, deliverance, etc.

Believe the truth of God's word without any doubt or reservation.

Christ nailed the shame and guilt of your past on the cross of Calvary. Your past is covered by the blood of Jesus Christ.

Believe that healing is available for all believers.

Chapter 3

Write down your visions, dreams, and the promises of God, constantly praying over them.

Position yourself for breakthrough by believing the word of God in your heart.

All breakthrough occurs by the empowerment of the Holy Spirit.

Ask God in prayer for wisdom, understanding, insight, and direction in all situation you encounter in life.

Ask God to guard your ways with his counsel, might, and knowledge by His Holy Spirit.

Meditate on God's word day and night, with the intention to obey it.

Approach God in prayer with the right motive in your heart.
Seek first the kingdom of God and His righteousness, and everything else shall be added.
Pray the heart of God by praying for lost souls, revival, and for the earth to be filled with his glory.
Pray for the advancement of the kingdom of God on earth.
Pray for God to use you in his miraculous work of deliverance, and setting captives free.
God's blessings in your life are not for you alone but for God's glory and praise, and for the advancement of his kingdom on earth.
Be humble at heart.
Recognize the greatness of God inside you, and the anointing of duplication.
When you encounter storms of life, ask God to show you the purpose in order to leverage the situation.
Ask God for strength to pass through the storms in your life.
Benefits associated with passing through trials of life include: patience, endurance, proven character, spiritual maturity, hope, and confidence.
Be still and know that God is always in control.
Always utilize the name of Jesus Christ in your prayers because, there is tremendous power in that name.
Overcome the valleys in your life by: identifying the valley, realizing your inability to do anything without God, operate in the prophetic by declaring life over your situation, asking the Lord to release his breath of life.
Tithing is holy and belong to God; and there are benefits associated to tithes and offering.
Ask God to provide you with good seed to sow on good ground.
Pray for the peace of Jerusalem
Pray for missionaries all over the world.

Chapter 4

God has great treasure for his children, and it is to impact the world for his glory.

You can take possession of God's wealth and riches by seeking first his kingdom and righteousness.

God has elevated you.

Conditions for restoration and blessings include: loving the Lord your God with all your heart, walking in his ways, and keeping his commandments.

Generating money mostly require a skill of some sort. This skill requires a careful deliberate process of learning and listening to the voice of God.

Recognize that no knowledge is wasted or lost.

The substance of who you are as a Christian, reside inside you.

The supernatural God abides in you.

Learn to hear the voice of God by reading and meditating on the word of God.

The Holy Spirit is our comforter, advocate, intercessor, counselor, strengthener, standby, revealer of secrets, reminder of all things, and much more.

You cannot operate in the ministry effectively with signs and wonders without the Holy Spirit.

Chapter 5

The devil's mission is to steal, kill, and destroy. The good news is that, Christ came and destroyed his works, and has given us abundant life.

The devil begins his destructive agenda from past generations.

Ignorance is a tool the devil uses against Christians.

God has set before you, blessings and curses; he encourages you to choose blessing and life for yourself and bloodline.

God has given you the power to tread on serpents and scorpions, and over all the powers the enemy possesses, and nothing will hurt you.

Curses and iniquity transfers to the third and fourth generations; while blessing transfer to a thousand generation.

The good news is that you can break curses from your life.

Victory is guaranteed in all spiritual battle you encounter in life

People who hate God are cursed.

As a Christian, you have the mind of Christ, and no curse or enchantment against your life will prosper.

Stand fast therefore, in the liberty wherewith Christ hath made you free, and be not entangled again with the yoke of bondage (Galatians 5:1).

WORKS CITED

i   Stephen O. J. By the rivers. On by *the rivers* [CD]. Abuja, Nigeria: Higher Dimension Music.
ii   Schnoebelen, W. (1994). *Blood on the doorposts: An advanced course on spiritual warfare.* Ontario, CA: Chick Publications.
iii   Goodrick, E. W. and Kohlenberger, J. R., III., The strongest NIV exhaustive concordance (Grand Rapids: Zondervan, 2004) 1501.
iv   Towns, E. L. (2008). *Theology for today.* Mason, OH: Cengage Learning.
v   The King James Study Bible commentary
vi   Entwistle, D.N. (2010). *Integrative Approaches to Psychology and Christianity: An Introduction to Worldview Issues, Philosophical Foundations, and Models of Integration.* Eugene, OR: Cascade Books.
vii   Goodrick and Kohlenberger, 329, 1546.
viii   Ibid., 376, 1583.
ix   The King James Study Bible commentary on James 5:14-15 (First reference Exodus 15:26, Primary reference James 5:14-16; cf. Matthew 19:14) 1944 & 1945.
x   Akhagbeme J. (2009). I am healed. [Unpublished Song].
xi   Goodrick and Kohlenberger, 1554, 1598.

xii Ibid, Isaiah 60:1-3; 239, 240, 2436, 2437, 3883, 5586. The word "Glory" in Greek is *doxa* which is closely related to the word in Hebrew *kābôd*. Ibid., 1422, 1542.
xiii Ibid., 1377, 1407, 1514.
xiv Ibid., 1429.
xv Ibid., 1502.
xvi Ibid., 1551, 1552, 1561, 1562.
xvii Dr. Malone, H., *Shadow Boxing: The dynamic 2-5-14 strategy to defeat the darkness within*. Lewisville, TX: VLM.

If you have been blessed by this book, we want to hear from you. Please, feel free to write or email your testimony to us.
May the Lord richly bless you.
Prayers that Produce Results: Praying the Word of God
JOA Ministries Publication

JOA Ministries
P.O. Box 490
Prosper, TX 75078

joaminsitries@gmail.com
www.joaministries.com
www.twitter.com/Joaministries
www.Facebook/Joaministries
YouTube/JOA Ministries

AUTHOR BIOGRAPHY

JOSEPHINE AKHAGBEME IS THE FOUNDER of JOA Ministries, which exist to empower the body of Christ through teaching of God's word, music and books; committed to equipping ministers and ministries through supplies of bibles, Christian literature, and equipment. She is actively involved in Missions, and Inner Healing/deliverance ministry with her husband, Bon; have five children and reside in the state of Texas. She is an Author, song writer, and poet. Her books include: Blessings of the Seed, and Your Right is Paid For.

She is a graduate of Liberty University, Lynchburg, VA, with Masters in Human Services Counseling – Marriage & Family, and Bachelors in Religion.

She is a recipient of the highly competitive DFW Public Service Excellence Award, State of Texas – 2014.

> *"However, I consider my life worth nothing to me, if only I may finish the race and complete the task the Lord Jesus has given me – the task of testifying to the gospel of God's Grace" Acts 20:24 NIV*

Additional Resources from Josephine Akhagbeme

BLESSINGS OF THE SEED

DECREES, DECLARATIONS, PRONOUNCEMENTS, BLESSINGS AND curses, agreements, covenants, conclusions and results are all made in the spiritual realm, which eventually are carried out and made manifest in the physical realm. Seed here refers to children and grandchildren, the fruit of your womb or lineage. God has given every parent a supernatural ability to bless or to curse because "Death and life are in the power of the tongue, and they who indulge in it shall eat the fruit of it [for death or life]" (Proverbs 18:21). You may be in a physical prison; you may not have had an opportunity to have parents release blessings upon you. You may not be feeling holy or adequate enough, or so you think. As a parent, a guardian, a caregiver, or a mentor, no matter who you are, God has divinely placed you as an authority to declare these blessings, and He will honor every word you release in faith in the name of Jesus Christ.

YOUR RIGHT IS PAID FOR

WHEN THE DEVIL WHO IS the destroyer attempts to steal, kill and destroy your Properties, Relationships, Children, Marriage, your Vision or your Walk with the Lord, you have the authority to stop him from proceeding based on the victory on the cross of Calvary by Jesus Christ. You can stand upon God's Word confessing it and believing in its entirety. Your right to good health, your deliverance from oppression, your breakthrough, your financial freedom; Your right to living your full potential on earth, is already paid for by the blood of Jesus Christ.

You might have lost your physical or spiritual freedom. You might be bound by the devil through drugs, sexual addiction or whatever you are struggling with, there is hope. God has something better for you.

This book will show you how to take back what the enemy has stolen from you, how to claim your family back to the Lord, how to keep the victory, your deliverance, and your authority through the power of the WORD in prayer.

Poem titled "People of my Kind" written by Josephine Akhagbeme

Made in the USA
Charleston, SC
02 December 2016